Inside the Revolution

A VOLUME IN THE SERIES

Anthropology of Contemporary Issues

EDITED BY ROGER SANJEK

A full list of titles in the series appears at the end of the book.

Inside the Revolution

EVERYDAY LIFE IN SOCIALIST CUBA

Mona Rosendahl

Cornell University Press

Ithaca and London

First published 1997 by Cornell University Press
First printing, Cornell Paperbacks, 1997

Library of Congress Cataloging-in-Publication Data

Rosendahl, Mona.
Inside the revolution : Everyday life in socialist Cuba / Mona Rosendahl.
p. cm. — (Anthropology of contemporary issues)
ISBN 0-8014-3381-9 (cloth : alk. paper). — ISBN 0-8014-8412-X (pbk. : alk. paper)
1. Socialism—Cuba—Palmera. 2. Cuba—History—Revolution, 1959– —Social aspects. 3. Palmera (Cuba)—Social conditions. 4. Political culture—Cuba—Palmera. I. Series.
HX160.P35R67 1997
335.43'47—dc21 97-16517

Printed in the United States of America

Cornell University Press strives to use environmentally responsible suppliers and materials to the fullest extent possible in the publishing of its books. Such materials include vegetable-based, low-VOC inks and acid-free papers that are recycled, totally chlorine-free, or partly composed of nonwood fibers. Books that bear the logo of the FSC (Forest Stewardship Council) use paper taken from forests that have been inspected and certified as meeting the highest standards for environmental and social responsibility. For further information, visit our website at www.cornellpress.cornell.edu.

Cloth printing 10 9 8 7 6 5 4 3 2 1

Paperback printing 10 9 8 7 6 5 4 3

Contents

Abbreviations

ANAP Asociación Nacional de Agricultores Pequeños. The association for small farmers, private and collective.

CCS Cooperativa de Créditos y Servicios. An association of private farmers, which gives them certain advantages when they need state loans or in buying equipment.

CDR Comités de Defensa de la Revolución. Neighborhood committees that guard and care for a barrio or village.

CPA Cooperativa de Producción Agropecuaria. A cooperative of small farmers who work their land together, sell the produce to the state, and share the profits.

CTC Central de Trabajadores de Cuba. The labor union, which organizes all employees at a workplace.

EMA Empresa Municipal de Agricultura. A state company that handles the production and distribution of agricultural products.

FMC Federación de Mujeres Cubanas. The women's federation, which organizes all women over the age of fourteen in Cuba.

PCC Partido Comunista de Cuba. The Communist Party, the only party in Cuba.

UBPC Unidad Básica de Producción Cooperativa. A kind of cooperative that has been created on former state farms.

UJC Unión de Jóvenes Comunistas. The youth organization of the Party.

Acknowledgments

Throughout my work on this book, many people have given me help and support. I particularly thank all my friends and acquaintances in Palmera, who shared much of their lives and many of their ideas with me. They made me realize that it is true that the inhabitants of this part of Cuba are, as the saying goes, especially warm and hospitable. Working in a foreign environment can be stressful and difficult, but the frustration and vulnerability that I sometimes felt during my stay in Palmera were cushioned by the affection people showed me. They received me with much generosity and accepted my sometimes strange Swedish ways with good humor. My neighbors at Los Edificios made me feel at home by including me in their daily activities. The girl I call Nena, who was nine years old when I met her, visited me almost every day during my fieldwork and taught me a lot about life in Palmera. She also introduced me to her family, which became, and still is, "my family" in Palmera. My workmates at the local office of the Ministry of Culture shared many laughs but also many serious discussions with me and have continued to be my friends through the years.

Many of my colleagues at the Department of Social Anthropology, Stockholm University, inspired me during my work on the manuscript, often during small talk in corridors or over a cup of coffee, but also in the Research Seminar and the Gender Theory Seminar, where parts of the manuscript were discussed. A special thanks goes to my friends and colleagues Eva Evers Rosander, Eva Poluha, and Annika Rabo, who read the manuscript at different stages, and to

Irène Svensson, who not only gave me good advice during a difficult stage in my fieldwork but also read and commented on the manuscript.

My colleagues in the Research Seminar at the Institute of Latin American Studies, Stockholm University, taught me a lot about Latin America in general and gave me a context for my study. The director of the Institute, Weine Karlsson, provided me with the contact at the Ministry of Culture in Havana that later led to my receiving a research permit and pursuing fieldwork in Palmera. He also made it possible for me to finish the manuscript and has helped and supported me throughout.

I am very grateful to the staff at the Ministerio de Cultura in Havana, who helped me obtain a research permit, and to the representatives of the ministry in "my" province, who introduced me to Palmera. Thanks also to the representatives of the Poder Popular and the Party in Palmera, who arranged the practicalities of my stay.

Annika Jagander at the Swedish Embassy in Havana, with her cool efficiency, made life easier for me during the preparations for fieldwork. She became a good friend with whom I continually discuss the intricacies of Cuban society.

Funding for my fieldwork was obtained from Humanistisk-Samhällsvetenskapliga Forskningsrådet, the Vega Foundation, and Sarec.

M. R.

Introduction

Cuban socialism has been scrutinized by scholars and political commentators since April 1961, when Fidel Castro openly announced that Cuban society was socialist. No social anthropological studies have been conducted, however, since the work of Oscar Lewis and his team in the late 1960s (Butterworth 1974, 1980; Lewis, Lewis, and Rigdon 1977a, 1977b, 1978).[1]

Soon after the victory of the so-called rebel army in 1959, the new government introduced radical changes to Cuban society, such as land reforms, nationalization and socialization of private property, and a literacy campaign. The U.S. embargo, beginning in 1961, forced Cuba into deeper and deeper dependency on Soviet aid.[2] Although Cuba struggled to maintain its independence, the Soviet model of socialism became an increasingly more important influence on Cuba's political and economic organization and its political ideology. The introduction of socialism has also had a profound effect on the lives of the people of Cuba. In 1988–1990, when I did anthropological fieldwork in the small municipality of Palmera in the south of Cuba, socialism was still hegemonic. By the beginning of

[1]Yvonne Daniel's book (1995) is based on fieldwork in Cuba but focuses on the rumba.

[2]Cuban authorities always use the word *bloqueo* (blockade) when talking about the U.S. government prohibition on commerce and other official relations with Cuba that began in 1961. The blockade is still in effect and was strengthened by the "Torricelli Act" of 1992.

the 1990s, however, the ideas of Marx and Lenin were pushed to the background and the more humanistic ideas of José Martí,[3] which had been important in the early 1960s, were once again highlighted. Nonetheless, socialism is still the only official political ideology in Cuba today, and it continues to be a strong normative guideline for most aspects of social life. The one-party system remains the basis of the country's political and administrative structure.

At the end of my fieldwork, in the summer of 1990, the era known as the *período especial* (special period in time of peace) began. The Berlin Wall had fallen the year before, and the Soviet Union was crumbling. These events affected Cuba's economy in drastic ways, by reducing the imports of oil and other goods by about 80 percent (IRELA 1994) as the former socialist countries in Eastern Europe and the Soviet Union began to demand hard currency and market prices for their goods. Cuba started on a path of reducing expenditures and building up economic self-sufficiency in as many regions of the country as possible. From 1990 to 1994, the economic situation continuously deteriorated and the black market grew exponentially. In 1993–1994, aspects of capitalism entered Cuba through the back door when the government depenalized the possession of dollars for all Cubans, encouraged joint ventures with companies from other countries, introduced some one hundred occupations as "private enterprises," and allowed a new type of cooperative to be established. All this, of course, affected the household economy as well as the political and social aspects of Cuban life.

My focus in this study is Palmera, a municipality of some thirty thousand people who live in several villages and small towns. It is their experience of Cuba's political ideology that will be recounted. It is their interpretations, their actions and reactions, and their attitudes that will be analyzed.

Most of my work in Palmera was done in the late 1980s, when the Cuban people had a fairly high standard of living and when loyalty to socialism and the government was strong. Yet I think my descriptions, dating from that time, are still valid in many ways. In July 1993

[3]José Martí (1853–1895), a poet, politician, and revolutionary, is considered the father of the Cuban revolution. He stands for humanism, national independence, and human dignity.

and May 1995, I revisited Palmera and witnessed firsthand the changes in Cuban society. I discuss some of these changes in the epilogue.

Among the questions I asked before starting my fieldwork in 1988 were these: What does a strong, unified, and hegemonic ideology mean to people who experience it every day of their lives? How is socialism presented to such people, and how do they react to the ideology? What other ideas, values, and attitudes do people hold that are not directly related to the hegemonic political ideology? How do these ideas coexist with the ideology? I was also interested in whether attitudes toward socialism differed among different social categories—men and women, young and old, more or less educated, and so on.

I use the term "ideology" here in a very broad anthropological sense, following what John Thompson (1990:44) calls "the neutralization of the concept." This contrasts with the classical Marxist view of ideology, which is used in reference to class-based societies and defined either as "false consciousness"—a set of ideas used by a dominant group to cover up the real relations of power in a society—or as "a system of ideas based on class position." In Marxist terms, Cuba is a classless society in which very few workers own their means of production and almost everyone works in a salaried position for the state. Existing differences in prestige and occupational position do not give rise to explicit group interests. A global definition of ideology as "the general process of the production of meanings and ideas" (Williams 1977:55), however, is too broad. Here I define ideology as a set of ideas that deals with society and social relations and that tells people "what exists, what is good, and what is possible" (Therborn 1981:27).

I use three approaches to look at political ideology from the Palmeran point of view. The first approach is to examine what I call the official ideology, the "systematic body of values, norms and beliefs" (Cohen 1979:90) originating in Marxism-Leninism and presented to the people by their leaders as the true and ultimate interpretation of and guideline for society. Cuban socialism depicts a set of ideals regarding the structuring of society and the values, ideas, and rules governing how these ideals should be achieved. Cuban socialism also has strong moral overtones that affect not only the formulation of practical politics but also the process whereby a human being is changed into a *hombre nuevo* (new person). This official ideology originates from a working-class perspective but is now presented as "universally valid" (cf. Williams 1977:66, quoting Marx's *German Ideology*). It can be seen as a Weberian ideal type, that is explicitly formulated, uniform, and well known to all leaders and most party members and indeed taught to them, but which is not always in accordance with events in real life. Traveling down through the political hierarchy, official ideas and messages are also given different slants in different situations and by different leaders.

The second approach is to examine the ideology as it is experienced in everyday life. In this context ideology can clearly be seen as a process in which collective memories, history, and personal experiences shape ideas and views of society. People interpret, accept, or reject the ideas presented by their leaders in accordance with their own experiences. The ideology changes those who live with it, but they in turn also change the ideology through their own relationships, experiences, and ideas. People at times use the official ideological discourse to formulate and reformulate their experiences, but they also draw their own conclusions based on other ideas.

The third approach is to analyze how socialism in Palmera is blended with, coexists with, and overlaps with other conceptions. I will discuss two different complexes of ideas that are extremely important in the daily life of Palmera, namely, those surrounding reciprocity and gender. These ideas are not part of the official ideology, but they affect the way all Cubans, leaders and others alike, think about and act in response to the dominant ideology. They are also of interest because both complexes can be seen as parallel to and in some ways contradictory to socialism, although both have also been integrated into and found new forms in Cuban socialist life.

A large part of my discussion is based on the emic view of socialism—what people call "the revolution"—a concept that refers to present-day Cuban society, as well as to the historical events from 1959 on and the ideas that are part and parcel of them. In my view this is a valuable standpoint from which to study political ideology, and especially so in Cuba, because it brings out the interplay between the hegemonic, unified, and "closed" official ideology and its diversified, flexible, and open "popular or folk versions." This view of socialism is not predicated on a unified, well-organized set of totally compatible ideas, but rather on multiple versions as they exist in any culture's representations of everyday life; "There is room here for choice, for alternative contructions, for creativity" (Keesing 1987: 372).[4] These representations of society are inspired by, but different from, the official ideology. Since the popular versions of ideology draw upon "common-sense knowledge and understandings of society" (ibid.:377), they are presented by local leaders as well as by people who are not politically active. This view of ideology also emphasizes the creativity and activity of people, which are vital to the understanding of ideological process (cf. Scott 1985).

This view is quite different from the official Cuban view of political ideology, which naturally accords with the orthodox Marxist-Leninist perspective. Cuban intellectuals do not wish to define socialism as an ideology since, as they see it, the term should be used only in relation to the bourgeois capitalist ideology.

An anthropological study of ideology is not complete without an examination of practice—the actions and reactions through which people communicate, enact, and revise ideology. It is difficult, if not impossible, for any anthropologist to know what people "really" think and feel. In Cuba this is even more difficult because of the hegemony of socialism. There are rules, explicit and implicit, about criticizing official policy. Cubans are not permitted to openly criticize socialism as a political system, which puts a constraint on ideological discussions even in private, especially with foreigners. To understand the ideas and feelings of others, one must observe and analyze what people are doing and saying, thus including practice in the process of shaping ideas.

This book provides an ethnographic analysis of socialist political ideology in Palmera and the processes of creating, recreating, denouncing, strengthening, questioning, and enforcing it. My presentation incorporates discussion of many events and statements I witnessed in Palmera so as to provide as complete a picture of this complex process as possible. Since there are very few empirical descriptions of everyday life in Cuba, I also believe these descriptions have an intrinsic value in bringing into focus beyond Cuba a society

[4]Roger M. Keesing (1987) is here referring to the concept of folk models.

that is still largely closed off to the outside, especially the Western, world.[5]

I have used pseudonyms for all places and people, except for well-known political personalities. To keep the identities of my informants truly hidden, I have sometimes given the same person different names in different contexts and altered details of situations. For the same reason I sometimes also use vague expressions such as "a man" or "a woman" and have refrained from presenting "whole persons" (i.e., letting the reader get to know an individual, his/her environment, ideas, and ways of life in, for example, a life history).[6]

The Cuban communist party, the local government, and the national mass organizations represented in Palmera form a backdrop for the ethnographic study that follows. I provide here brief profiles to which the reader may want to refer on occasion.

El Partido Comunista de Cuba/PCC (the Communist Party of Cuba) formulates the ideology and policies of the country, makes final decisions, and holds ultimate power. It operates in the centralist tradition with a selective membership, closed meetings, and a hierarchical structure in which higher levels or posts have power over lower levels or posts. The smallest unit of the Party is the *nucleo* (the base group), constituted by the *militantes* (members of the Party) at a workplace. The next level is the *municipio*, which includes a municipality committee and a *buró ejecutivo* (executive committee). In 1990, the buró ejecutivo in Palmera consisted of seven members—three full-time professional members and four others. The buró ejecutivo handles daily decisions in the municipio; the three professionals, the first secretary, and two other secretaries direct this work. The municipality PCC is subordinate to the provincial Party and in turn to the national Party. Members of the PCC are nominated by other members or apply themselves by letter. If they are accepted, they must undergo a one-year apprentice period and thereafter may be accepted as full members. Every year an evaluation is made of all

[5]There are several journalistic accounts of life in Cuba. Most were published shortly after the revolution, for example, Yglesias 1968 and Sutherland 1969. An interesting more recent report can be found in Miller 1992.

[6]An example of such a life history is *Nisa: The Life and Words of a !Kung Woman*, in which Marjorie Shostak (1990) also discusses the ethical dilemma of exposing a person so fully to the audience.

members, and those who do not measure up to the standards of a militante may be sanctioned.

The Unión de Jóvenes Comunistas/UJC (the Youth Organization) is also selective and organized hierarchically. Members may be active up to the age of thirty and thereafter must either quit or apply to join the Party. Some UJC cadres already have double membership in the Party; for example, the first secretary of the UJC in Palmera is a member of the Party buró ejecutivo.

After the Party, the most important political organization in Cuba is the Poder Popular (People's Power), the government, formed in 1976. The Poder Popular is organized hierarchically in the same manner as the Party. The smallest unit is the *circunscripción* (the constituency), which includes a local neighborhood or a village that elects a delegate. These delegates make up the *asamblea municipal*, which makes decisions on practical administrative matters in the municipality. The delegates of the asamblea municipal elect representatives to the *asamblea provincial* and also a *diputado* (representative) to the asamblea nacional.[7] The asamblea municipal also elects a *comité ejecutivo* with (in Palmera) five full-time professionals and eight other members who oversee day-to-day operations.[8] The Poder Popular has overall responsibility for all practical matters in the municipality, including education and the budget of the municipality. It receives a budget from the higher levels of the Poder Popular, which is used within the municipality. In Palmera it is often difficult to separate the responsibilities of the Party and the Poder Popular since the two work hand in hand and the Party often rules on matters that belong under the control of the Poder Popular. In effect, the Poder Popular executes decisions made by the Party (cf. Jørgensen 1983: 38).[9] In 1990, *Consejos Municipales* were introduced at an intermediate level between barrios, villages, or towns and the municipality (cf. Bengelsdorf 1994:163-66).

The mass organizations of Palmera are arranged hierarchically in

[7]In 1993, representatives to the national and provincial assemblies were elected for the first time in direct elections.

[8]The number of persons in the comité ejecutivo depends on the number of inhabitants in the municipality.

[9]Bård Jørgensten's article (1983) is a summary of his master's thesis (1980), which is written in Norwegian.

the same manner as the Party and the Poder Popular with local, municipal, provincial, and national levels. The main characteristic of the mass organizations is that they are not selective; any Cuban who falls within their sphere of operation may join. The largest mass organization is the Comités de Defensa de la Revolución/CDR. Members of the CDR are supposed to guard their villages or blocks, to attend to the physical condition of their neighborhoods, and to check on "antisocial" behavior. These organizations also function as neighborhood social clubs.

The Federación de Mujeres Cubanas/FMC (the Women's Federation) organizes all Cuban women over the age of fourteen. It has very much the same function as the CDR but is directed only at women. The Pioneros organizes all schoolchildren in grades 1 to 9. A branch of the UJC, it is meant to provide children with an ideological education. It also organizes recreational activities for children.

Another mass organization is the Central de Trabajadores de Cuba/CTC (the labor union). All administrators and workers at a workplace are in a local branch of this national organization.

The Asociación Nacional de Agricultores Pequeños/ANAP (the Small Farmers' Association) organizes both private farmers and those who belong to cooperatives. The ANAP is both a political and a practical organization that provides information on production methods as well as socialist ideology.

[1]

Limones, Palmera, Cuba: The Field and the Fieldwork

I arrived in Limones, the capital of the municipality of Palmera, on a scorching afternoon in mid-October 1988. Coming to the hill approaching the town that would be my home and workplace for almost two years, I was overwhelmed by the view—the sun glittering in the deep blue sea, the beach with white sand, the palm trees, and the forest-clad Sierra Maestra mountains, shifting in color from green to lilac to black, far away at the horizon.

Limones has about three thousand inhabitants. It has many of the functions of a small town but the feeling of a village. It is situated on the very edge of the Caribbean Ocean and spreads northward to the foot of the mountains. Most people live in single-family houses with shaded well-kept gardens where fruit trees and colorful bushes grow. Many families have pigs, hens, or perhaps a goat. Most houses have two or three bedrooms, a dining/living room, and a small kitchen. The houses are open: one door at each end of the house permits a cool breeze to blow through during the hot days. The windows have venetian blinds made of wood, but no glass.

During the late 1980s, three apartment houses were built in an area that was immediately named los Edificios. These buildings are five stories high and contain one-and two-bedroom apartments. People earn the right to these apartments by being exemplary workers. In 1988, my building was home to a doctor, a clerk, a teacher, a construction worker, a cook, a telephone operator, a carpenter, a taxi driver, and a lawyer, among others. Some came from bigger cities in the province or from Havana, others from mountain villages in the municipality, from bad housing in Limones, or from other towns. Most of the residents were young or middle-aged, and many had children.

Because of the shortage of housing, most people in both houses and apartments lived crowded together. Families often divided their living quarters or built extra rooms when children grew up.

During my fieldwork in 1988–1990, Limones gave one the impression of well-being and was bustling with people, movement, and sounds. The day started around six o'clock for those who had long journeys to work or who wanted to take advantage of the cool mornings. A little later women and children walked to the milk shop to fetch the daily ration of milk for children and old people. Around eight o'clock children left for school and office workers set off to work, some in cars but most on foot. The mornings were usually quite still but were sometimes punctuated by muted sounds drifting through venetian blinds—someone shouting a greeting or calling a workmate to hurry up or a mother scolding her child for goofing around.

Later in the day car horns honked, music and laughter drifted from open doors and windows, people carried on loud conversations, and radios blared from porches and balconies. There were always people in the streets, on motorbikes with side-cars, on horses, and in trucks, buses, olive-green jeeps, and a few private cars. Animals sometimes escaped from back yards and were then chased by screaming and laughing children. Well-dressed people, the women often in bright colors, walked slowly along the streets, stopping for a greeting, flirtation, or a short talk with an acquaintance. They walked in the shade, and the women often carried umbrellas to shield themselves from the scorching sun. Children, in red or yellow school uniforms, ran, laughed, and bumped into each other in the yards of the primary and junior high schools or played *pelota* (baseball) on the back streets.[1] A barber, whose shop was a chair under a large tree in front

[1]All children in Cuba are incorporated into the Pioneer movement when they enter school at six years old. At that time they belong to what is called the Pioneros Moncadistas and wear blue scarves with red trousers or skirts as their school uniform. In junior high school they pass on to the Pioneros José Martí and wear red scarves with yellow trousers or skirts and white shirts. Children in all grades vote for their

of his house, almost always had customers. At the hairdresser's shop women talked about the latest news while sitting on the porch waiting for their hair tint to settle or for a manicure. The restaurant and the coffee shop had many visitors when there was something to serve. The planned economy and the scarcity of goods made the availability of items erratic; shops or restaurants could not order what they needed but had to wait for goods to come to them from other levels of the commercial organization. Queues often formed outside the town's stores. The general store sold household articles, cloth, shoes, clothes, writing materials, and other items. El Mercado Paralelo sold nonrationed items on the free market, such as soap, cigarettes, and rice. The food store distributed rationed goods at low prices—rice, beans, spaghetti, lard, and so on—as well as some "free" items, but its shelves often gaped empty. La Pescadería (the fish shop) was, in spite of its name, most crowded when it sold rationed meat every second week.

Sometimes a bride and groom dressed in wedding clothes would wait outside the marriage office and schoolchildren would crowd into the library. On the square, people visited the tiny bookshop; the office of the Dirección de Cultura; the artisan shop, which sold artifacts made by the local handicraft industry; and a small kiosk that served coffee and tea and sold cigars and rum when it was available. On the main street, there were constantly people waiting in front of the buildings or in the reception area of the Party and the Poder Popular to ask for help from or to lodge a complaint to the administrators and politicians working there. The closed-in area of the staff of the Fuerzas Armadas Revolucionarias (Revolutionary Armed Forces) of Palmera was also here. In small houses along the main street, people worked in different administrative organs, such as the statistical unit, the labor administration, the economic department of the Poder Popular, and, close by, the school administration.

At night voices were more quiet, but televisions played loudly, crickets buzzed incredibly loudly, and frogs croaked. People visited friends and relatives, and groups of men gathered in parks and under the strong lamp at the food store to play dominoes. Just before nine

---

school, grade, and class leaders and have meetings to talk about schoolwork and leisure activities.

o'clock on the nights of the popular Brazilian *telenovelas*, a steady stream of people left their houses to visit neighbors with functioning TV sets.[2] The big movie theater on the main street showed films every night. If they could get hold of some beer, people would have birthday parties at their houses, to which they would invite friends and relatives. Every now and then there would be communal fiestas under the beautiful big mango trees at the plaza called Los Mangos. These fiestas were often arranged by some mass organization or by the local cultural administration and offered live music and sometimes a barrel of beer. People, old and young, danced, talked, drank, and joked in the warm, soft Caribbean night.

Palmera is a small and rather poor municipality. Its thirty thousand inhabitants live in a few coastal villages or small towns and in villages and settlements in the mountains. The climate is tropical, and the daytime temperature in Limones stays at about thirty-four to thirty-five degrees Centigrade almost all year. In the mountains, the climate changes and becomes cooler. Many people in the big city consider the municipality a "backward" place, and sometimes Palmerans refer to themselves as *guajiros* (a derogatory word for *peasant*). Palmera has a young population; 55 percent are under the age of twenty-five, 35 percent between twenty-five and fifty-five, and 9 percent older than fifty-five.[3] The region is historically significant because it is in the part of the country where Fidel Castro and his men began the revolutionary war in 1956. Many of the older inhabitants took part in one way or another in the struggle.

The people of Palmera exhibit all shades of skin color from white to black and many combinations of facial features. As in other parts of the Oriente (the eastern part of Cuba), there are more blacks in Palmera than in the country as a whole, but most people call themselves *mulatos* or *mestizos*, signifying that they are a mixture of black, "Indian," and white.

Most Palmerans work in agriculture, cattle raising, and forestry.

[2]Cuban television has shown telenovelas, romantic Brazilian TV series, two or three times a week for many years. Telenovelas are immensely popular and engage the whole female population and most men, who follow them with vivid interest and discuss characters and events.

[3]Municipal statistics from 1989.

This work is done either on private farms, in cooperatives, or on the state farms, which employ 47 percent of the total workforce.[4] Private farmers are sometimes organized in a type of cooperative called a *cooperativa de créditos y servicios*/CCS, which gives them advantages when they want loans or to buy equipment for their farms. CCS farmers have to sell their produce to the state, but otherwise they operate like other private farmers. Most have diversified production that includes raising some animals (cows, pigs, goats) and growing tubers, fruit, and coffee. The other type of cooperative is the *cooperativa de producción agropecuaria*/CPA, in which members own and work the land together and also share the profits from produce. They have the same manner of production as the CCSs but sometimes on a larger scale.

The second biggest work sector is services, which are concentrated mostly in Limones and the other coastal towns, where people work in shops, a few restaurants, and coffee shops (11 percent) and in transport (2.5 percent). Medicine is one of the most important social services in Cuba today, and the medical staff of Palmera is large (8 percent). Palmera has two hospitals with a total of eighty beds, one hospital is in Limones, and the other one is in the extreme west of the municipality. Since 1986, there have also been about fifty *médicos de familia* (family doctors) and nurses in every corner of the municipality, however remote. These doctors live and work in small white houses that are easily recognizable since they are all built in exactly the same style, with a water tank on the roof, living quarters for the doctor upstairs, and a clinic downstairs. The doctors are often young and fulfilling their *servicio social*, the two to four years of social service people with higher education must perform as an obligation to the state. These doctors often come from other parts of the province or the country, and some become quite important in the villages where they work, not only as authorities on medical matters but also as organizers of cultural, social, and political events.

A significant percentage of the population, especially women, works in education (11 percent), both as teachers and administrators. There are no high schools in Palmera, which means that all high school students must go to boarding schools in other parts of the

[4]Municipal statistics from 1989.

province. Junior high school children who live in remote areas of the mountains also go to boarding schools.

There is no heavy industry in Palmera, but in 1989 a dairy plant was built to pasteurize milk and make yogurt. Both women and men also work in workshops that produce household utensils, clothes, and ornaments and in local bakeries (4 percent).

Finally, some people, especially women, do not work. There are two reasons for this. First, most available jobs in the municipality are in agriculture. Both the authorities and the women and their husbands view these jobs as unsuitable for women since they require heavy work and long commutes. Second, the municipality does not provide communal child-care facilities. Women with small children who do not have female relatives close by or who cannot afford to pay a woman to care for their children are unable to work outside the house.

The normal workday is eight hours, between 8:00 A.M. and 6:00 P.M., with two hours, between 12:00 P.M. and 2:00 P.M., for lunch and a siesta. Those who are *dirigentes* (leaders), political or otherwise, work longer days and have no fixed hours. Many others work fewer hours, sometimes because of slack work discipline but mainly because of uncertainties with transportation and commerce. Those who go to work by bus often have to wait for hours because the vehicle is missing tires or other parts. Housewives often take long lunch breaks or leave work to stand in line when desired goods arrive in the shops.

In Palmera, as in the rest of Cuba, there are no classes in the Marxist sense of the word. Except for some private farmers and a few private artisans who own their own means of production, all Cubans are employed and paid by the state. There are, however, differences among occupations in their salary, status, prestige, and power. Medical doctors and political leaders have the highest status in Palmera. Other high-status occupations are chauffeur/mechanic, for men, and teacher, for women. In the case of doctors, their salary coincides with their status, but political leaders often receive only modest salaries. The lowest-status occupation is agricultural worker, which pays very little.

In 1976, after the reorganized administrative division of Cuba (see Rassi 1981), Palmera became a municipality with the borders it has today.[5] Until the mid-1960s, this region was part of a much larger administrative area and played a very peripheral role in it. Most people lived in the mountains on small fincas, as tenant farmers or squatters. In the 1960s a road was built which connected the coastal towns and villages.

Today most of the villages in *las lomas* (the hills), as the Sierra Maestra mountains are called, have fairly good services, including a shop, bus transportation every day when the roads are passable, electricity, a family doctor, and a primary school in the vicinity. Dirt roads lead up from the coast to the mountains, and when it rains the roads look more like river bottoms and trucks and buses have trouble passing. Most people living in las lomas therefore ride horses or mules or walk, even when traveling long distances.

Small farmers live in villages, in dispersed settlements with one or two families, or in cooperatives. On the steep mountain slopes, cooperatives and private farmers cultivate the staple food of the municipality, what they call *viandas* (tubers)—yucca, yams, sweet potatoes, malanga, and plantains.[6] They also pick oranges, lemons, guava, avocadoes, and mangoes to sell to the state warehouse. Of prime importance to the Palmeran peasants and cooperativists is their main cash crop—coffee.

The many rivers that run through the municipality are of vital importance. Small power installations provide electricity to villages and settlements. Women, sitting waist deep, wash clothes in the river. Children, grown-ups, and animals bathe in the river, and one of the most popular pastimes in the summer is to immerse oneself in the water while drinking rum and talking to one's friends.

Limones became the main administrative and political center of the region after the revolution, when people began to come down from the mountains to take advantage of the new work opportunities and better services in the coastal villages. Quite a few Cubans also arrived from bigger cities to do specialized jobs, since even now few

[5]There are fifteen provinces in Cuba and between eight and twenty municipalities in each province.

[6]In non-Cuban Spanish *vianda* means "food" (Collins Spanish Concise Dictionary 1990), which says something about the importance of tubers in the Cuban diet. For most Cubans, a meal without some *vianda* is not a real meal.

natives of Palmera have advanced educations. Today, the leaders say, Palmera is acquiring its own identity, and the aim is to have as many positions as possible filled by people from the municipality.

My choice of Cuba as a field site stemmed from an interest in ideology and local politics that I had pursued in earlier fieldwork among Swedish factory workers. Among these workers I identified a duality of ideals and influences rooted in both the workers movement and the bourgeois society in which they lived (Rosendahl 1985). This made me want to study a society with a strong, unified ideology to examine what it meant to people in everyday life. I thought that a socialist country like Cuba would be an appropriate place to study what in my research proposal I called "ideology in everyday life."

When I began to read about Cuba I had only vague notions about the country. I knew about Fidel Castro and the revolution and had read Che Guevara's *Reminiscenses of the Cuban Revolutionary War* (1971). I also had vivid personal memories of the missile crisis in 1962, which my father feared would lead to a world war. As a person with left-wing ideas I admired the Cuban people for making their own revolution. Overall, I saw the country's social development as positive. I had never regarded socialist countries as ideal societies, however, and two visits to the Soviet Union had left me with more negative than positive impressions.

My first trip to Cuba in 1986 led to no specific research contacts, although I did acquaint myself with the country, from Havana in the North to Baracoa in the East, as I traveled widely by bus and train. In Havana I walked hundreds of miles and got to know the life of the streets quite well. I also learned to understand fast Cuban Spanish, which is different from the *castellano* I had studied in Sweden.

When I returned in 1987, the Research Department at the Ministry of Culture agreed to be my sponsor in Cuba. I had expressed a wish to do fieldwork outside Havana and preferably in the Oriente. The easternmost part of Cuba, the Oriente has had a very interesting history since colonial times and was the "cradle of the revolution," which started in the Sierra Maestra mountains in 1956 (Pérez 1988). When I met with the head of the provincial Ministry of Culture in 1987, he suggested that I check out Palmera as a field site. I saw no reason not to accept the invitation since I had no knowledge of other parts of Cuba that would suite me better. Furthermore, I was afraid that if I did not accept his recommendation, it would delay or make my fieldwork impossible. In November 1987, I spent one week in Palmera with the local representative of the Ministry of Culture, a young woman, who took me around the municipality in a small truck driven by her chauffeur. She also introduced me to her friends and to leaders in the municipality. I readily accepted Palmera as my field site, and my hosts at the Ministry of Culture promised to arrange for a research permit. After months of preparation in Cuba and Sweden, I at last had a field site.

In 1988, I received funding for my project, and in September I set out for Cuba. When I arrived in Havana, my research permit was not ready and my stay in Palmera was not yet arranged. After four weeks in Havana, I set off on a thousand-kilometer trip across the island, in my brand-new red Niva, a Soviet jeep.

On 14 October I arrived in Limones and was installed in my new two-room apartment. I was received by representatives of the Poder Popular and of the Ministry of Culture of the municipality, who helped me with both practical and research matters. The first secretary of the Party, the most powerful man in the municipality, said that I was welcome to take part in everything in Palmera except meetings of the Party.[7] This did not surprise me because I already knew that all meetings of the Party are closed to everyone except members. Otherwise, I had access to most parts of Palmeran society. I participated in ceremonies and official gatherings, I took part in five municipal assemblies and several meetings of the FMC, CDR, CTC, and ANAP, as well as the meetings of my "own" CDR and FMC. I was welcome to accompany others doing voluntary work and developed friendships with people in my barrio, in the local Cultural Administration, and eventually in other parts of Palmera. The Cultural Administration became a source of much information. I visited it almost every day to chat with the people working there and to

[7]When writing about the Communist Party of Cuba, I have adopted the emic expression "the Party." Since it is the only political party in Cuba and no one ever qualifies it by talking about the "Communist" Party, I use "the Party" with a capital *P* to emphasize its uniqueness.

receive help in practical matters. I also visited a friend in the Poder Popular many times a week.

Unlike the usual contacts in most fieldwork, my principal contacts in the beginning were not the "marginals" or the "deviants," as Michael Agar (1980:85–86) calls them, but the official representatives of society—leaders of different kinds, militantes, and officials. This was only normal since I could not live in the community without sanctions from the leaders. Only slowly did I come into contact with other people, some of whom were marginals. I do not think that my relationship with them was hampered by the fact that they knew I was also friendly with the leaders, but I am sure that some people avoided coming into closer contact with me for this reason.

My neighbors were all very generous and welcomed me by giving me small gifts, promising to help me, and inviting me to their homes. I went to fiestas and danced, with a liberal interpretation, *cubano* style, drank beer and rum, and joked with my new friends. Nena, a nine-year-old girl who lived in my building, visited me almost every day to tell me about her school, talk about her friends, and play cards with me.

During the first weeks I mostly walked around, trying to get my bearings. This astonished my new neighbors, who could not understand why someone who owned a car would voluntarily walk anywhere.

People to whom I was introduced or who stopped me in the street all started off by asking how I liked Cuba, how long I had been there, and how long I would stay. Then they asked me about Sweden, saying that they knew of Olof Palme, who "was a great friend to Cuba."[8] Most women also asked if I had children and looked disappointed when the answer was negative. My new acquaintances had me talking so much about myself and Sweden that I began to wonder if I was ever going to get to ask *them* about Cuba. When I left my apartment, the children playing between the buildings greeted me by shouting *¡Sueca, Sueca!* (Swede!), giggling uncontrollably.

[8]Olof Palme was the prime minister of Sweden from 1969 to 1986, when he was assassinated. He had a keen interest in international issues and made a great impression on the Cubans when he visited Cuba in 1975 and made a speech in Spanish (see Goñi 1987: chap. 5).

After about one month in Limones, I heard that people were going on voluntary work to plant coffee bushes in the mountains. I asked if I could join in and was told that "I did not have to," "it wasn't necessary," "it was hard work," and "did I *really* want to go." When I persisted, their raised eyebrows told me that they did not think much of my abilities to plant coffee bushes. I worked hard because, like many fieldworkers, I was glad to feel useful. Afterward I understood that my willingness to participate had been my ticket into the community. People I met on the street stopped me to say that they had seen me working hard and congratulated me on my zeal, implicitly hinting that they had not expected a Sueca, an academic, and a "capitalist" to be able to do manual, hard work or to want to do something "for the revolution."

I took part in volunteer work brigades many times, mostly picking coffee. One day I met a young man beaming with pride who told me that he was the vanguard agricultural worker that year because he had picked 2,100 latas of coffee (42,000 liters). I realized what that meant when I went to the mountains to pick coffee. Between slipping on the steep hills, getting entangled in lianas, roots, and spiderwebs, sweating, and swearing, I often could not pick more than two to three latas in a day.

In the beginning of my fieldwork, Cuban Spanish was difficult for me. I knew Spanish, but the Cuban dialect was hard to understand. Much of my linguistic limitations also reflected my lack of understanding of the local context and culture. I soon learned that problematic or difficult phenomena were often discussed in indirect ways, making it hard to know whether it was my understanding of the language or of the culture that failed me. Late in my fieldwork, when I was quite sure of my language abilities, I was at a meeting when the discussion got highly animated. I turned to my neighbor and said that I did not understand one iota of what people were saying. He smiled and answered: "You are not supposed to understand anything." The discussion focused on a scandal involving one of the leaders in the municipality, and everyone was treading on very thin ice, alluding to old knowledge of the matter and voicing exceedingly vague opinions.

Some of the leaders in the community, who knew of my interest in local politics, took me to political meetings and ceremonies, and when the leaders had no other transportation, my Niva was a ticket to participating in meetings in las lomas. I learned something about the structure and organization of Cuban society at these meetings, although I still understood neither all of the language nor the cultural codes. My contact at the Poder Popular also arranged interviews with the leaders of the mass organizations and other institutions in Palmera.

Shortly after my arrival, I got into a fierce discussion with my new friends Juana, José, and Arturo, all militantes, and Ramón, not a militante, about democracy and the pros and cons of glasnost. That was the first time, but definitely not the last, that I heard militantes wholeheartedly defend their Party, Fidel, and the revolution. When I told them that I thought it was wrong that Cubans could not go abroad, they explained about the U.S. embargo, the trips overseas that Cuban workers can win for their exemplary work, and the wish most Cubans have to build their country rather than to travel. When I criticized the government for censoring newspapers and television, they explained that Cuba does not have censorship. Naturally, a political line has to be followed, they said, but people can say whatever they like. Furthermore, they have the mass organizations and the Poder Popular, through which they can take part in political decisions. And, they emphazised, Cubans are certainly more free than people in most other Latin American countries. They also explained that there is no need for other parties because the PCC governs with the support of the people and in a way that has given Cubans all the good things they have. I was frustrated almost to tears because my Spanish was not good enough to explain what I really thought. Finally, Ramón, the non-Party member, ended the discussion by telling his countrymen that I naturally had another point of view since I came from Sweden. Afterward I was afraid that I had said too much, that they would see me as an arrogant European and a counterrevolutionary. But we would have this discussion many times more, and it became more subtle as I learned more Spanish and understood more about Cuban society. Perhaps also during the two years of our acquaintance, my friends started to rethink some of what they had taken for granted before.

Older people told me about the times *antes* (before the revolution) and the hardships they had to endure then. They also proudly told me about how they helped the rebel army during the revolutionary war in 1956–1959 and that some of them had met Fidel, Camilo Cienfuegos, Celia Sánchez, and Che Guevara.

I found out that despite their leisurely ways, many people were working very hard, both in their ordinary jobs and their voluntary work—planting or picking coffee, building schools or other public works, or planting trees. They also had to attend military training every month. I was incorporated into the CDR in my apartment house and the FMC and heard people constantly refer to "the revolution," meaning everything from society at large to government to the entire historical period after 1959.

Whenever I caught on to a Cubanism or answered back in a cocky way, my friends laughed, shook their heads, and said: "Ah, Mona, sabes demasiado" (Oh, Mona, you know too much).[9] I had become Mona, instead of La Sueca.

In this phase of my fieldwork, I was presented with an idyllic picture of Cuba and Palmera. Although there were complaints about the shortages of goods, the bad transportation, and the lack of housing, most people seemed like "good revolutionaries," having totally internalized the socialist ideology. As I spent more time in Palmera, however, I saw more and more of what was below the surface. I had good contacts with both men and women, but my access to male groups and places frequented by men was more restricted. I often sat in kitchens chatting with women but very seldom joined the men in "the street" or at the dominoes table. This was not because they stopped me from taking part in activities but because my presence turned the whole situation into a show of manliness, which made it less interesting as a source of information. My information about men's discourse on sex, gender, and women is therefore limited, although I sometimes talked to men about these matters when we were alone. In mixed company (several Cuban men and women), the conversations consisted mostly of joking, tales about what the participants had experienced lately, or gossip. Slowly I developed close relationships with a few women but also a couple of men who shared with me the latest gossip about personal and, at rare times, political

[9]Bård Jørgensen, a Norwegian geographer, reports that he elicited exactly the same reaction. See his paper that deals with the Poder Popular (1980:101).

scandals. My contacts covered the whole age range, from children to old people, although except for a few of my friends' teenage children, I had, few informants of that age.

After some months, officials who earlier had invited me to all kinds of meetings (except those of the Party) started to withdraw their support and no longer provided me with information as willingly, leaving me worried and feeling abandoned. What was happening? Would I be able to continue my fieldwork? I even thought about going home. Although I was well aware of the ideal of "detached involvement" in fieldwork, I knew from my work in Sweden that it is difficult to be detached. A part of me could analyze the situation from outside, but my feelings of insufficiency and lack of support were overwhelming.[10] I still do not know what actually happened, but I am almost certain that someone in the political hierarchy felt that I was getting too much information and ordered a screen put up.

After writing about my situation to an anthropologist friend in Sweden with a lot of experience in Latin America, I got an answer that helped me turn my fieldwork around. "Don't bother with the leaders," she wrote. "There are others who are just as interesting and not so afraid of losing their face or position." After feeling sorry for myself a bit more, I started to turn to my neighbors and friends who were not leaders of any kind.

What I eventually found, of course, was the "back stage." Many of the impressions I gained during the earlier phases of my fieldwork still held, but now they became more nuanced. People in many ways agreed with and felt grateful for the progress in equality and the standard of living that the socialist government had achieved. But there was also deep discontent with the lack of democratic rights. There were people who wished for a more pluralist political structure, more freedom of speech and in writing, and a more flexible leadership. Some of them were totally against the system, while others, most in fact, just wished for change within the socialist system.

I also saw and heard of indifference toward the official society,

[10]Hortense Powdermaker (1966:58–59) jokingly tells about a similar situation and ends with a truth that I think is also valid in my case: "Panic is a state of unrelatedness."

which manifested itself, for example, in people working no more than three to four hours in full-time jobs when they could get away with it and in pilfering and, worse, in outright stealing of scarce goods at workplaces. It also manifested itself in a disinterest in the society at large and a lack of responsibility and initiative.

Slowly, my female friends started to talk about their situation as women, to complain about the machismo that still exists and makes them feel insecure about their status as wives, especially when their husbands are running around with other women "en la calle" (in the street), as they put it. They felt a quadruple pressure to be good revolutionaries, good mothers and housewives, good workers, and attractive lovers. They complained that their men never helped around the house and with the children. We also laughed together, commenting on the men passing in the street and gossiping about who was seeing whom at the moment.

I tried to get permission to conduct a survey of the people in Limones. The questionnaire that I showed the authorities had questions about social relations and the standard of living, but also about politics. It was discussed by the leaders of the municipality, in the province, and at the Ministry of Culture in Havana and contacts were made with the University of Santiago, but ultimately my request was turned down. I was told that surveys like mine could be conducted only by Cuban institutions and when authorized by the political organizations.

When I arrived in Cuba, I had a long list of projects that I wanted to undertake during my fieldwork—interviews, questionnaires, sociograms. Most of these activities were not possible, in part because scheduling was not as rigid in Cuba as in Europe and I had to learn to be more flexible. I also had to learn that in Cuba no one likes to say no, especially to a guest, and therefore many of my suggestions were, as I saw it, approved when in reality there were such delays that I eventually had to accept them as refusals.

Since I was interested in how ideology is spread, I wanted to be a participant observer in the primary and junior high schools in Limones, where I knew that ideally all teaching would be carried out from a socialist standpoint. I never had an opportunity to observe in a classroom, however, since I never received a response to my request during the whole period of my fieldwork. I did know several teachers personally and was allowed to conduct some interviews with other teachers.

I did not begin formal interviews until well into the long period of fieldwork. In total, I conducted about thirty interviews, most with a tape recorder. Most of my informants were eager to talk to me, but I also detected a formality in their responses that was not present when we chatted. People were eager to tell about their lives but did not readily voice opinions or ideas about contemporary society in interviews. Informally, however, people were very outspoken on all topics.

In January 1990, after fifteen months of fieldwork, I returned to Sweden for six months to analyze my data and to try to get some distance from my experiences. When I returned to Palmera in the fall of 1990, a lot had changed. Both Eastern Europe and the former Soviet Union were turning into market economies and now demanded hard currency for their exports to Cuba. People were aware that "el período especial" would be a period of many hardships. In an effort to increase economic self-sufficiency, people were urged to plant their own gardens, and many white-collar workers were sent out to do agricultural work. Gas rations were cut by 50 percent, and electricity had to be rationed. Industries were partially or totally shut down, and magazines and newspapers reduced the frequency of publication or, in some cases, ceased publication. To get the country through this difficult time, politicians talked even more than usual about the importance of everyone sacrificing for the revolution.

It was a delight for me to see all my friends and to be once again in this beautiful part of the world. During this last period in the field, my work was more focused as I conducted interviews, participated in union and CDR meetings at various locations, and tape recorded meetings and official gatherings. This time I did not have a car and it was much more difficult to move around, so I stayed in Limones a lot or took buses, which were even more undependable than before because of the shortage of gas and parts.

During a visit to Havana as I was starting my last month of fieldwork, a representative of the Ministry of Culture told me that my work permit had expired. The representative also told me that the authorities in Palmera and the province were dissatisfied with the handling of my fieldwork. Although the people at the ministry assured me that the authorities were not dissatisfied with *me*, I was greatly disappointed. I felt extremely upset, even betrayed. I returned to Palmera to find that the goodwill of the local authorities had diminished. I was once again assured that there were no ill feelings toward me but that they felt that the ministry had not handled my situation adequately. The apartment I had been renting, which everyone had assured me I could have for as long as I wanted, suddenly was urgently needed for other people. What made this experience most frustrating was that I did not understand what was happening and no one explicitly explained it to me. I felt let down and complained to my friends. They were ashamed of the treatment I was getting, and many of them assured me that they loved and respected me. I should not bother about what the authorities were doing; this was typical, they said. How many times do you think we are abused by the capriciousness of power, they asked. No one had so clearly and emphatically expressed their feelings of defenselessness before. Suddenly my whole fieldwork came into clearer focus. I had reached a stage all fieldwork should eventually reach—when the anthropologist and the informants share personal feelings that cannot easily be expressed in words or on an intellectual level alone.

I believe now that there were several reasons for the sudden turn of events. There were obviously political difficulties between the different levels of decision making. Some officials may also have been worried, starting earlier, because I had such a thorough knowledge of the municipality and by how difficult it was to control my activities and the information I received. The main reason, however, probably was the new, difficult situation in Cuban society. The leaders knew that the economic situation would deteriorate and maybe feared that people would become increasingly dissatisfied. This was not a good basis, as the leaders saw it, for an anthropological investigation. Later I also learned that at the beginning of the special period the Party tightened its control of its militantes, who were told not to associate too freely with foreigners. So, when my three visa-free months, which all Swedes in Cuba enjoyed up to 1995, were over, the authorities saw no reason to renew my work permit.

I had all the material I needed, but in retrospect I can see that these events affected my analysis of it. It confirmed a feeling that I already had of the use of power in Cuban society as capricious, tacit, fluid, and thereby much more difficult to handle. It did not, however, change my general impression of Palmeran society.

The ethics of doing fieldwork in a society like Cuba are not very different from those required in other fieldwork. Most anthropologists tell about problems with authorities, with entering the field, and with deciding what to write about and what not to mention. There are, however, some special aspects associated with the centralist political structure of Cuba and what I call the political intolerance that may make life more difficult for the fieldworker as well as for those who interact with such a researcher. This makes everyone involved in an exchange of information acutely aware of what can be said, what cannot be said, and whether it should be said. Thus, the fieldworker, more than in other fields, has to rely on guesses, reading "between the lines," and deductions to understand what is happening.

There is also another problem with doing fieldwork in a socialist, centralist society, and that is the prejudices everyone from nonsocialist countries carries with them. Although I tried to be as open-minded as possible, and although I was rather receptive to much in Cuban society, I could not help carrying with me expectations of repression, restrictions, secret police, control, and censorship. Some of this certainly existed in Cuba during my fieldwork, but the society was also much more open than I had expected. I never felt overtly watched or controlled. For some time, this made me believe that there was no monitoring in any way of my actions. Later I understood that little of my activities escaped the watchful eye of the authorities. People I met and got to know seldom showed any fear of expressing their often very critical opinions. This made me think that the self-censorship that I witnessed in some Palmerans was exaggerated and cowardly, until I understood that it was only a great skill in judging the limits and contexts of criticism that made some people so outspoken.

In writing this book I have agonized over what to write and how to express it. My first concern has been to protect my informants, most of whom are also my friends. My second concern has been to balance my description and analysis so as to demonstrate my deep love and affection for Cuban society while also recognizing the less positive traits that exist in this society, as in all others.

Limones, Palmera, Cuba

It is difficult as a foreigner to criticize Cuban society. One of my gravest concerns has been how Cubans will judge this book. For so long outside critics, for political purposes, have ethnocentrically judged Cuban society unjustly and without understanding it. Many Cubans therefore put up their guard in response to any criticism. A good friend of mine in Palmera said many times while I was doing my fieldwork that he was looking forward to reading my book, but only if I discussed both the good and the bad sides of Cuban society. I hope my friend will find both the good and the bad sides in this book and that he will understand that my view of his society has been offered with sincerity.

[2]

To Give and Take: Redistribution and Reciprocity in the Household Economy

The national economy of Cuba is characterized by its redistribution and planning. Since 1961, when the socialist system was introduced, the Cuban economy has functioned as a tightly controlled field guided principally by the Party and monitored by local organizations. The data in this chapter deal with the period before 1990, when the Soviet Union discontinued its special trade arrangement with Cuba and the economic crisis began. An update on the economic situation since then is given in the epilogue.

Other than a very small group of *particulares* (own-account farmers, artisans, hairdressers, manicurists, and so on), everyone is employed by the state or state organizations, and farmers sell only to the state.[1] Profits from all products sold go to the state exchequer and are then redistributed in different ways—through free medical care, inexpensive drugs, free education, and subventions on food and other goods.[2] People do not pay income taxes but do pay fees to the

[1]Today many more occupations have been introduced as particulares, and "private" farmers' markets are allowed.

[2]For a discussion of Cuba's national economy, see Brundenius 1984 and Zimbalist 1989.

mass organizations; to the Party, if they are members; and to the militia. These fees go to support these organizations, but also in part to the state. The economy of the state is planned both long and short term, and the provinces and municipalities have overall budgets drawn up by higher political levels. Within the guidelines assigned, local governments can use the resources as they see fit, for education, sports, or construction, for example.

Although the Cuban economy provides most citizens with a comfortable standard of living, there is also a considerable bureaucracy. The lack of goods is something Cubans struggle with every day. Although rationed basic foodstuffs and other necessities can almost always be obtained, everything else is either lacking because of deficiencies in distribution or is in scarce supply. The scarcity results from the lack of foreign currency, which in turn stems from the difficulties in trading with Western countries because of the U.S. trade embargo on Cuba. Foreign currency must thus be used for the most important items, such as raw materials for industry, so that there is not enough money to import goods people would like in more abundant supplies.

In everyday life, the planned economy is evident principally in the rationing system and the *emulación socialista* (the socialist competition). But an informal economy, with "gray" and black markets, also exists, as well as a system of reciprocity and barter, which brings people together through the constant giving and receiving of articles and services (see Hart 1973; Smith 1989; Gudeman and Rivera 1990; Humphrey and Hugh-Jones 1992).

The Rationing System

The core of the Cuban household economy is the rationing system, which guarantees every citizen basic goods in equal amounts and at very low cost. Every person has two *libretas* (booklets)—one for food and one for clothes and other household items—in which rationed items are listed and checked off when purchased. Foodstuffs that can be bought on the libreta are those that are the most often consumed, such as rice, beans, lard, sugar, detergent, and soap.[3] Each person also is allowed one-third of a loaf of bread each day, which costs 12 centavos (15 cents).[4] Rationed items can be bought for approximately 9 pesos per month per person (U.S. $12), not counting cigars and some special articles for children. Every second week each person

[3]*Libreta items and their prices in 1990*

Product	Amount/person/month	Price (pesos)
Rice	5 pounds	1.20
Beans, peas, lentils	40 ounces	0.41–0.54
Lard	1 pound	0.30
Cooking oil	1 pound	0.40
Sugar, brown	5¾ pounds	0.46
Sugar, white	¼ pound	0.11
Coffee	4 ounces	0.20
Condensed milk		
7–13 years	10 tins	3.00
65– years	4 tins	1.20
Fruit purée		
0–13 years	15 tins/jars	2.25–3.75
Tomato purée	2 tins	0.60
Noodles	1 pound	0.20
Canned meat	1 tin/3 months	0.36
Cigarettes	4 boxes	1.20
Cigars	4 cigars	0.60–0.80
Toothpaste	1 tube	0.65
Detergent	3 ounces	0.06
Soap		
for washing	1 bar	0.25
for bathing	1 bar	0.20–0.25
Cleaning rags	2/family	0.40
Kerosene (1 person)	3.5 gallons	1.12
Kerosene (5 persons)	9 gallons	2.88
Alcohol	5 litres	0.50

Information from the local shopkeeper in Limones. Cf. Pérez Lopez 1989.

[4]When transforming pesos to U.S. dollars, I have used the rate 1 peso = U.S.$1.25 (approximately). This is not really a valid measurement, however, since the peso is nonconvertible. The best way to assess the value of the peso is to compare salaries and costs.

also gets one-half pound of beef, which costs 30 to 40 centavos (40 to 50 cents).

Many people buy all the items in the libreta and sell or exchange those they do not use. Libreta household products can be bought once a year. This list includes such items as sheets (one set for 2.20 to 3.00 pesos), work shoes (one pair for 6 to 10), dress shoes (one pair for 15 to 30), cloth (4 meters for 1.20 to 17.50), towels (one for 2.50), and underpants (four for 1.20 to 2.20). Many people feel that the clothes offered on the libreta are so unattractive that they do not want them. Other items, such as underpants and socks, are perenially in short supply. When people speak about the scarcity of goods, they say that goods do "not come" in sufficient quantities, which emphasizes the perceived and real distance between consumers and the system of central distribution. Insofar as this system is nationwide and state controlled, entities at the local level have very little control over distribution. The shops receive goods from higher levels and cannot order more themselves if something is sold out. This leads to constant vigilance awaiting the "coming" of goods and a complicated informal queuing system. The use of the libretas for household products is organized in a complicated way, so that there are specific buying days for each person, thus giving people access to goods at varying times. Finally, there is also the Plan Jaba, which gives precedence in the ever-existing queues to women who work outside the home.

In addition to rationed goods, some foodstuffs (vegetables and tubers), canned goods, clothes, and household items are sold *por la libre* (on the free market) at the parallel state market.[5] These articles are subject to some market principles of demand and supply, so that vegetables, for example, are cheaper when there are a lot available. Other items are always much more expensive on the free market. Rice, for example, costs 1.50 a pound (compared to 24 centavos when it is rationed) and peas cost 2.15 a kilo (compared to 37 centavos a kilo when rationed).

[5]After fall 1990, all items became rationed and household items have not been sold at all for several years.

Four Households and Their Economies

Data on the economies of four households were obtained through interviews with the women of these families.[6] These women usually buy the goods and are responsible for the household economy. Since none of the women made budgets, it was impossible to get exact figures, but almost all the women could estimate rather closely how much they spent each month on different items. The two father-and-mother households have joint household economies, but in some other families the men keep most of their salaries and contribute only a portion to the women for household expenses. Three of the women said that "there is always enough money for our needs," and the fourth claimed that "there is never enough money for our needs." None, however, felt any need for more control over her domestic economy. Three of the families lived in apartments, and one lived in a small house. All had the installment payments for housing deducted from their salaries, together with a sum for other items bought on installment.

Single-Person Household

Juana is rather unusual in Limones in that she has lived alone since she was divorced. She has a good job and earns 265 pesos a month (U.S. $331). Her former husband left her his libreta when he moved out, and she buys some of the items on this libreta as well as her own. Juana estimates that she uses about 10 pesos for rationed food and household items and 1.20 for meat but says that she does not always buy all the allotted alcohol and kerosene for the stove. She also buys about 20 pesos of food on the free market, mostly fruit, vegetables, and tubers. She eats many of her lunches in the canteen at work, which costs her about 40 to 50 centavos (50 to 60 cents) for each meal. Previously, she saved 45 to 50 pesos a month, and when she has paid for her furniture and refrigerator, she will start saving the same amount again. Because of her job, Juana has a telephone, which is a real luxury and costs her quite a lot each month. She is a

[6]For a comparison of a household economy in an urban working-class Argentinian setting, see Jelin 1991b.

prominent person in Limones and receives many gifts of food from friends and neighbors, as well as from her big family, which has animals and fruit trees. Juana's monthly budget would look approximately like this:

Food	42.00 pesos
Housing	45.00 pesos
Electricity	8.00 pesos
Fees	5.50 pesos
Telephone	11.00 pesos
Furniture	17.00 pesos
Refrigerator	25.00 pesos
or	
Savings	45.00 pesos
Total	153.50 (173.50) pesos

This means that Juana has about 100 pesos left from her salary when she has paid for her monthly expenses. She spends much of this 100 pesos on clothes. She likes to dress well and buys cloth, which her sister sews for her, or clothes in the free-market shops.

Household of Mother, Father, and Two Children

Papito, the father, in this household, is an administrator and earns 190 pesos (U.S. $241) a month. Anita, the mother, is a teacher and earns 283 pesos (U.S. $353) a month. The children, nine and fourteen years old, are both in school. The family has four libretas, since all children get a libreta the day they are born. The family buys all the rationed items it is allowed and spends about 25 to 30 pesos on these items. They also buy food on the free market—canned items, vegetables, fish, ice cream, and so on—for about 30 pesos. Anita saves some money each month, and both parents occasionally save a sum for the children. They bought their television set for cash but have paid for a refrigerator and their apartment on installment. They have many relatives and friends in the neighborhood and receive food as gifts or buy it inexpensively from them. Anita also raises chickens and sometimes a pig at the finca of a relative. Their approximate monthly budget is as follows:

Food	60.00 pesos
Housing	50.00 pesos
Electricity	10.00 pesos
Fees	6.75 pesos
Refrigerator	14.00 pesos
Savings	40.00 pesos
Total	180.75 pesos

This family lives rather inexpensively. After they have spent their monthly fixed amounts, they still have about 290 pesos left for clothes, recreation, and other items.

Household of Mother, Father, and One Child

In this family, the father, Jesús, earns 230 pesos (U.S. $287) a month as a cook, while the mother, Gloria, earns 118 pesos (U.S. $147) doing manual labor. Their nine year-old child is in school. They buy everything they can each month on their three libretas and estimate that they use 20 pesos for that, which is probably a low estimate. They also buy about 30 pesos of food from the free market. Jesús can also buy leftover food inexpensively at work. He eats every second day at work, paying the full canteen fee. Gloria also eats at her workplace, for 25 to 35 centavos a meal (35 to 45 cents). They save occasionally, but Gloria says that they are wasteful with their money. They spend a lot every month on cigarettes and smoke two packs each day. Gloria is often sick and has to stay home from work. On these days she is paid only 40 to 60 percent of her salary. They sometimes receive gifts from relatives and friends, but not often. The biggest aid to their domestic economy is that Jesús can buy food cheaply at work and sometimes can take leftovers home. Their budget would look approximately like this:

Food	50.00 pesos
Housing	47.00 pesos
Electricity	10.00 pesos
Fees	7.75 pesos
Furniture	22.00 pesos
Transport	12.00 pesos
Cigarettes (free market)	77.00 pesos
Total	225.75 pesos

After this family has paid for all its expenses, it has about 120 pesos left.

Household of Mother and Two Children

Graciela has one thirteen-year-old child who is in school, while her eighteen-year-old son is now working. She has a manual job earning 100 pesos (U.S. $125) a month. Her son pays 40 to 50 pesos to his mother each month. He keeps the rest of his salary of 114 pesos (U.S. $132) for himself. They have three food libretas, and Graciela says that she buys the food for the three of them but does not use the full ration. Graciela estimates that she uses 15 pesos for libreta items but that she spends about 30 to 40 pesos a month for food, cigarettes, and other things on the free market. She very seldom buys any clothes or other items and is always pinched for money. The children's father sometimes pays when they need something special. Graciela seldom receives food from others and only occasionally raises chickens or pigs. Her budget would look like this:

Food	50.00 pesos
Housing	8.50 pesos
Fees	1.50 pesos
Refrigerator	30.00 pesos
Total	90.00 pesos

Graciela makes a very low estimate of her monthly expenses. She most certainly uses more money for food and other necessities. In this budget she has sixty pesos left for non-essentials, but Graciela often borrows money from friends and claims that she cannot pay required fees to her union and the mass organizations. The only way she can moderate her domestic economy, she says, is to reduce her food costs, which she does when possible.

From these examples, we can see that many people have more money than they spend. This is in part why dissatisfaction with the lack of available goods is probably the most common complaint that people in Palmera express about their life situations.

Good Food and Nice Clothes

The cost for food on the libreta is very low, but most families buy food on the free market and therefore use about 15 percent of their salary for food. In addition, they purchase beer and rum for parties.

Most people in Palmera like to eat well and a lot. They eat hot meals twice a day (rice, tubers, meat, fish, or anything else available). Rice and often beans are served in abundance with a little meat or fish to go with it.

Food also has a symbolic value which is related to society and gender. Having enough to eat is associated with a good life and a good society. Eating heartily, especially meat, connotes masculinity, whereas cooking and serving plenty of good food is connected to female gender ideals. The female tradition of serving platefuls of food still persists in many families. The mother first serves the father a large plateful of food, then the sons, and then the daughters, who get less. Finally she takes what is left.

The favorite foods among most men (and many women) in Palmera are the traditional foods of the Cuban countryside, *macho asado* (roast pork), which is served mostly at parties, and yucca or yams.

The gendered importance of meat was illustrated by a bitter saying a female friend quoted to me: "El día de la carne es el día de los padres, porque los otros días son de madre." This is difficult to translate with all its connotations, but the closest is "The day of the meat [when the ration is distributed] is father's day, because all the other days are *de madre*" [which literally means "mother's day" but also means "terrible," "hellish," or "disappointing"].

Muñoz, an older man, once said to me in talking about the scarcity in the Cuban economy: "What we Cubans want is to eat good and dress well. Therefore it is difficult when we cannot get hold of clothes and good food." He explained that he, a manual worker, had his niece buy *guayaberas* (traditional dress shirts) for him por la libre in the city where she lives. They cost 60 pesos each, about half his monthly salary, and he paid her in installments. His wish to be well dressed made it worth the economic sacrifice.

As we have seen, food and clothes are indeed what people in Palmera generally spend most of their money on, the women buying cloth to sew for themselves, their children, and sometimes their husbands. People buy clothes on the free market or in *tiendas de amistad* (shops where imported goods are sold very expensively), or they buy them in the street from black marketeers. Some people also buy household appliances por la libre, but that is so expensive that few can do so. An electric fan, for example, costs 90 to 120 pesos depending on the size, a refrigerator 700 to 1,000 pesos, and a TV set 500 to 600 pesos. Instead, most people wait to win these articles in the emulación socialista, the socialist competition, which is open to people at all workplaces except those who have political appointments.

Emulación Socialista

Cuba's planned economy is closely connected to its socialist ideology. This is evident in the discussions about the need for economic versus moral incentives, which have been going on in Cuba for the more than thirty years under socialism. In the early 1960s, Che Guevara advanced the idea that good revolutionaries should not need economic incentives to work productively for their society (Deutschmann 1987: 159–168); the mere satisfaction of doing a good job for the revolution should be enough. It was evident, however, that this did not work very well, and economic rewards, so-called *estímulos* (stimulis), were introduced.

Under this arrangement, the state distributes desirable articles to the central union, which in turn distributes them to the municipality branch unions those in the central union feel have done good jobs. The branch union leader then awards the articles to different local unions, from which a group is elected to choose the persons who have earned the most merits and therefore will be awarded the article. The article is not awarded free of charge but may be bought at a much lower price than in a shop or on installment. A small electric fan, for example, costs 40 pesos compared to 90 pesos on the free market.

This arrangement, of course, leads to conflicts among workmates when someone feels unfairly treated. While I was in Palmera, the biggest conflicts arose when housing was at stake, since shortages are severe. The conflicts usually arise over the way merit points are counted. Every worker collects merit points by doing voluntary work, by being a conscientious worker, and by being a good workmate. Some workers think they have not received all the points they should and that they therefore lose in the competition.

Sometimes foreign travel is also distributed as estímulos. One of my neighbors who had been a vanguard worker for many years was awarded a two-week trip to the Soviet Union. Everything for her and her husband was paid for, and they even got some money to buy winter clothes since the trip was in October. For most Cubans, this is the only way of ever traveling abroad.

Queuing

One of the most salient features of Cuban society today is its queues. Everywhere and almost constantly one sees people gathering, not in straight lines but in clusters. After a while, one learns to do like the Cubans and join a queue before even asking what is being sold. Some people do not like the queuing system and say that it is not necessary, but almost everyone who can uses it, not daring to wait, since desirable articles might then be sold out. Some people, such as teachers, however, cannot leave their jobs to stand in lines for hours.

The queuing is, of course, a result of the scarcity of almost everything in Cuban society, but it has become a great pastime as well as a habit. The rules of queuing are very well defined. Everyone arriving at a queue will ask for *el ultimo* (the last person) in a loud voice. This person waves a finger in the air. This "last person" then announces who is in front of him or her and maybe also the second to-the-last person, so as to guarantee that if he or she leaves for a while or drops out, the new person will know who precedes him or her in the queue. If the "last person" is not there when the new person arrives, someone else provides the information.

A queue is a place for conversation, jokes, and gossip, and those who have time to spare can enjoy themselves thoroughly. The queues are not always orderly, however. In Limones, the three days every second week when meat is distributed are a busy time for the salespersons in La Pescadería. The queues are enormous, and the police are often called in, to put men and women in different queues and to break up fights, which occur when discussions get too heated. The same ruckus occurs when perfume, underpants, or shoes come to the shop on the main street. When cloth arrives at the one time during the year when Palmerans may buy the four meters they are allowed, there is not always enough for everyone and the queues are at their most intense.

One Tuesday night, a couple of days before Marta "had her letter"—that is, before it was her turn to buy her ration of cloth for the year—she heard that there was a queue forming outside the shop. She changed to her street clothes, put on some lipstick, and walked over there. A few people were waiting, and a man had started to organize the queue, giving out little pieces of paper with numbers on them. Since Marta was early, she got a very low number, twelve, and was thus guaranteed that there would be cloth for her. The man told her to come back at one o'clock that morning to confirm her place in the queue. She went home and watched a popular telenovela, content that she had a good spot in the queue. At a little before one o'clock, she walked tiredly to the queue and confirmed her place once again. There were loud discussions between Marta and some other women who felt she had cheated them of their places, but she went home to sleep. For the next confirmation call, at six o'clock that morning Marta sent her daughter, who again confirmed their place. By now some people had dropped out, and Marta received an even lower number. During the day, she checked several times with the queue, and after lunch she went to the shop to stand in line herself. After a few hours she came out with her four meters of cloth, one piece for a friend of hers and two pieces for herself and her daughter.

In addition to queues, there are other ways to get scarce goods. Someone can bring along a friend's or a relative's libreta and buy for her. If the article is sold por la libre, some people buy as many items as possible and resell them to friends and relatives for the same price as they are sold on the free market. Many working women complain, however, that they never have the opportunity to buy popular items since they are always sold out when they have time to shop.

The "Gray" and the Black Markets

The queues are sometimes instruments of the gray market, which recirculates legal commodities. There are people, for example, who buy items in the official stores and then resell them privately to others at higher prices. Goods bought on the libreta that a family does not consume may also be sold or exchanged. There are even people called *coleros* (queue sitters), who are said to stand in every line there is and to make good livings on the articles they then resell. There are also legitimate libretas floating in the community that do not belong to the people who hold them. These persons can thus buy more than they use and resell the surplus to others, at a profit. These transactions are usually not made with friends or relatives since they would sever the reciprocal relationships that ideally should exist between them. More often these articles are offered to casual acquaintances.

The black market in clothes is especially widespread. Most people in Palmera want to be nicely dressed and like the modern, foreign clothes they can obtain from the *bisneros* (a slang expression for black marketeers). The bisneros operate in the bigger cities, changing money with foreigners to get hold of dollars, which until 1993 Cubans were forbidden from owning. The bisneros then get foreigners to buy clothes and sometimes other items at the Cubalse (the foreigners' shop), where Cubans usually cannot buy. They then resell these articles in the street at exorbitant prices.[7] A T-shirt that costs U.S. $2 to $3 in the Cubalse is sold for 50 to 60 pesos (U.S. $65 to $75) in the street. Jeans that cost U.S. $10 in the Cubalse cost 150 pesos (U.S. $200) or more in the street. Since most Cubans have more money than they can spend on the few items available in the shops, they can afford to buy these black market items every now and then.

Another illegal activity that is widespread is taking articles home from work. This can range from the rather innocent activity of pilfering light bulbs or paper to the much more serious crime of organized theft of construction materials or other high-value goods.

[7]During my fieldwork these prices *were* exorbitant, but compared with the prices on the black market in 1993 they are rather low.

Reciprocity

Marcel Mauss (1969) introduced the idea that the exchange of goods includes both an economic and a social component, which builds and reinforces social relations. Many others (Scheper-Hughes 1992; Smith 1989; Stack 1974) later discovered that the relations involved in giving, receiving, and repaying gifts is not only the basis of many traditional societies but also operates widely in contemporary, large-scale economic systems. Within many socialist planned economies, there exists an informal economic sector that depends in part on loans, gift giving, and the cultivation of reciprocal relationships (Evans 1993; Yang 1988). Reciprocity has always been important in Cuban society, but since the revolution and the introduction of socialism, new forms of reciprocity have developed.

In Palmera reciprocity is a vital part of the informal economy.[8] There is one form of reciprocity that is almost totally social and in which the monetary value of the articles, goods, and services subsumes a subordinate role to the creation and maintenance of social relations. At times there are no gifts involved in the transactions, just "symbolic capital" (Bourdieu 1977), via *cultura* (cultured behavior) that strengthens one's reputation as a "good person" within the context of an established relationship.

With other forms of reciprocity, the goods and services exchanged become a very important part of the household economy although the transactions also serve to cement and create social relations. Scarce goods can thus be exchanged and both parties profit. A friend of mine who maintained several hobbies, including photography and fishing, complained that these hobbies involved much work and even stress. But, he said, "through my hobbies I get many friends and they help me and I can easily *conseguir* [get hold of] almost everything." To him, his hobbies were also an investment in the future.

The acts of giving, receiving, and repaying gifts are clearly present

[8]Reciprocity in the form of work exchange and ritual gift giving are common in many Latin American societies (see Hugh-Jones 1992; Isbell 1978; Gudeman and Rivera 1990), but in my opinion the contemporary Cuban type of reciprocity more resembles the kind Carol Stack (1974) describes since it is not organized on the community level but more informally, although it still has rules and a structure.

in reciprocal relations in Palmera, but the way transactions are accomplished varies. When the economic aspect is more important, the repayment is swift and the gift is expected to be equivalent in value to the gift that is given. When the social aspect is the vital component, the gifts can be less equivalent in value, and the interval before repaying can vary greatly. The closeness of the relationship also makes a difference. Friends who have established relationships can allow themselves to exchange less symmetrical gifts, while looser acquaintances must follow more timely and symmetrical patterns in the gifts exchanged. Under certain circumstances, however, friends may have a reciprocal relationship that is mainly economic, and acquaintances may build a friendship through their mainly economic reciprocity. Repayment is extremely important. The person who does not repay is excluded from the relationship, or the nonrepayment is taken as a sign that he or she wants out.

Evidence of reciprocity can be found in all corners of what we might call the informal sector, the entire array of economic transactions that exist side by side with the formal state economy. These transactions involve the exchange of money, goods, and information in differing combinations.

Economic Aspect of Reciprocity

For most people in Palmera, having acquaintances with access to scarce items is crucial for success in procuring goods and is a constant preoccupation. The exchange that transpires very much resembles balanced reciprocity in Marshall Sahlins's (1972:194–95) terms, or what Caroline Humphrey and Stephen Hugh-Jones (1992) call barter, which they define more broadly than do most scholars.

I was once approached by a woman who wanted me to buy some clothes for her child at the Cubalse. We did not know each other well but had met and chatted in the street at times. She wanted to pay me in pesos for what I bought for dollars. Since this is a felony for both parties, I always refused such requests. I told the woman that I would buy her the clothes, which cost me a very small sum, but I gave them to her as a gift. She then said that she had a chicken at her mother's house and she would go there to get it and give it to me. I replied that she should keep the chicken, that I did not want anything for the clothes. Nonetheless, two days later she came with the chicken and presented it to me. In my eyes her repayment for my gift was much too much, but if she had bought the clothes on the street from a bisnero, she would have had to pay much more than the value of the chicken.

Every conversation in Palmera starts with a discussion of where one can buy something. The most common form of reciprocity, in which everyone takes part, is the giving, receiving, and repaying of information about the availability of various articles.[9] The scarcity of goods, the erratic distribution system, and the disorganization of the market make it extremely time-consuming to procure things. *Conseguir*, which literally means "obtain" or "procure," has become an activity of great importance in maintaining reciprocal relationships. Since there is almost always a scarcity of goods, people cannot just go out and buy what they want, even if they have the money. They have no choice but to enter into the process of *consiguiendo*. Thus, everyone is always on the lookout for articles to buy or advising others about where they can find what they are looking for.

Maria called Margarita from her office to talk about a problem at work. After having greeted one another, Maria started by telling Margarita that she had seen some nice suede shoes at a shop in a mountain village. "They cost thirty pesos and they come in your size four," she said. "Miquel is going there tomorrow. I can ask him to buy some for you." Margarita jumped at the opportunity and would look up Miguel and give him the thirty pesos. When she in turn gets news of something that she thinks Maria needs, she will tell her, and so the reciprocal flow benefits them both. This means, of course, that a person can also withhold information from others and give it only to preferred friends, thereby strengthening the relationship with them.

Another aspect of reciprocity is begging; it is not unusual and is considered acceptable among friends. The item asked for is often given since it is something the person who is asking knows that the

[9]Elisabeth Jelin (1991a:30) calls this "information capital," paraphrasing Pierre Bourdieu (1977).

giver can and might well give him. Some items are also asked for as a compliment, or to express interest, but are not meant seriously. Eva wore a pair of white tennis shoes when visiting her friend Maribel. Maribel admired the shoes and said: "Give them to me! I've always wanted a pair of white sneakers." Eva just laughed, saying that Maribel would have to cut her toes off to get her feet to fit in the shoes since her feet were so much bigger than Eva's. "Come on," said Maribel, "I'm sure they will fit." Both laughed knowing that Eva would not give away her shoes. Eva said, however, that she would ask her sister in town who had bought the shoes to look for a pair in Maribel's size.

When the begging is no longer considered acceptable—when someone asks too much or of the wrong person—it causes embarrassment or shame to the beggar and also to the person who has to say no. José was approached by a person who wanted to be given or possibly lent one hundred pesos. Quite upset, José afterward told me that he hardly knew the person, had not seen him for two years, and that, of course, he refused the demand. He felt embarrassed, mostly because the person was so forward and did not have the cultura to understand that one does not do such a thing. First of all, the sum was too large. One might lend or give a very good friend or a relative such a sum but definitely not an acquaintance. Second, they did not know each other well enough to support such a reciprocal relationship, and José did not want to develop such a relationship with the other person.

A short while after I moved into the barrio, I started to get visits from people who begged for different things, from plastic bags to pants or other clothes. Those who had already become my friends were embarrassed about this behavior and told me never to give anything to these people. They might themselves very well ask me for things, although always small items, but this was in the process of ongoing reciprocity, since they also gave me things, invited me to dinner, and helped me in many ways.

In all of these examples, an element of economic gain guides the relationship, but the transaction also has social implications. The context, the status of the people involved, and their relationship determine whether or not the exchange is successful (cf. Hugh-Jones 1992).

Social Aspect of Reciprocity

The more symbolic aspect of reciprocity in Palmera also involves gifts, but in this case their significance is more social than economic. Small gifts and loans constantly move back and forth between people, tying them more and more closely together.

When I moved into the little, spartan apartment where I lived during my fieldwork, a neighbor immediately came to visit with a glass of strong, sweet Cuban coffee. She welcomed me and said that if I ever had any problems or needed help with anything, I was to feel free to ask her and her family, who would try to help. After some days, she came knocking on my door asking if I could possibly spare a *cubalse* (a plastic carrier bag). Bags are scarce in Cuba, and cubalses, which are used for all purposes, are extremely popular and washed until they disintegrate. I gave her two cubalses, and she departed happily. This was the beginning of the kind of reciprocal relationship most people keep up with their neighbors.

Being generous and hospitable is a very important part of being a good person in Palmera (cf. Gilmore 1990:88; Herzfeld 1987). There is a saying Palmerans like to quote with pride, that the people of this region are especially warm and hospitable. Children are taught from their first months to be sociable, to kiss and talk, and to relate easily to others. By the time they are older, they have learned the socially correct way of entertaining a visitor and always bid a visitor to sit and offer him or her something to eat or drink.

This is part of the concept of having cultura, which can be translated as "being cultured" but which really means much more than that (cf. Gilmore 1980:59). The concept includes the notion of knowing how to behave toward other people, not being coarse or vulgar, and knowing the rules of social reciprocity.

Part of having cultura and being a good Cuban is being "happy," or at least acting as if you are. Many people said to me that they did not show their unhappiness to their friends and acquaintances, because "they are not the cause of it and should not be made to suffer for it." Showing too much suffering to the outside world causes embarrassment, which should be avoided at all costs, and demonstrates a lack of cultura. Showing suffering to a friend in private, is totally acceptable, however, and women at least do much serious talking about their problems and give advice to each other.

Having cultura also means being generous, especially with one's house and one's time. Very few people in Palmera would ever say that they have no time to talk to or see someone. They stop what they are doing when visitors come, or if the visitor is a close friend or relative they continue with what they are doing and invite the visitor to stay anyhow. This is partly because it would be very rude not to welcome visitors, but also because people do not enjoy being alone. Most Cubans live close to many people during their lives, with siblings and parents while they are unmarried and then with others, sharing a place of their own. Many people say that they cannot imagine living alone and that they do not like, almost fear, being alone.

When I arrived to visit the Martínez family, the door was half open to let in some cool air. Papito, the man in the house, was lying bare-chested on one of the beds. Excusing himself for not wearing a shirt, he got up and greeted me with a wave of the hand, exiting to put one on. Anita, his wife, shouted her hello from the kitchen. Nena, their eleven-year-old daughter, was washing the floor in the sitting room. She greeted me with a kiss in the air toward my right cheek, and using the respectful *usted* address, asked me how I was. Anita came out to the sitting room, kissed me on the cheek, and beckoned me to come into the kitchen. She was cutting yucca for lunch. Rice was simmering in a big pot. "Nena," she shouted, "fetch the stool from the bedroom for Mona." Nena brought it to the small, dark kitchen and invited me to sit. While Anita prepared the food, she gave me cold coffee, which she had left from breakfast. Papito came into the kitchen and, asking Anita if she had given me coffee, greeted me with a handshake. We talked a little about the carnival, which was to be held in the community the following weekend. Anita invited me to have lunch with them. I could not stay, and I said that I felt embarrassed because I ate there so much. "Don't talk rubbish," said Anita, "estás en tu casa [you are in your own house]" (cf. Herzfeld 1987). As I left, Anita gave me yucca and plantain to take home.

This scene includes many aspects of cultura that one encounters when visiting Cubans. Greetings are made either by kissing on the cheek or shaking hands. Although people may meet several times in a day, they always greet each other formally. Palmerans say that the custom of kissing on the cheek is fairly new there and that it was not done before. When people meet in the street they usually stop and shake hands or kiss, ask "How are you?" and exchange a few words, mostly about the welfare of the family or other friends. *¿Y Pepe?*, for example, is the ritual phrase for inquiring about someone. The equally ritualized answer is *Bien* (cf. Gilmore 1980:96). A throwback to the times when people used to shout to each other in the mountains is the greeting used to someone across the street—"*¡Ay-eeeeeeeeee, compay* (mate)!"—*compay* being the familiar word for *compadre*, the ritual godparent-parent relationship seldom referred to today. What is important, however, is not *how* a person greets but *that* he or she does so.

The offer of a seat and something to drink or eat is equally important when someone comes to visit. It is said that it does not matter what one offers as long as one offers something. A glass of water can be sufficient. If the host does not have anything in the house, which is not unusual since scarcity is the rule in Cuba, he or she makes excuses and says, "I don't even have coffee to offer you." Very often, though, a visitor is offered coffee, homemade juice, ice cream, and sometimes soft drinks or sweets.

As important as the offer of something to eat or drink, the guest must be invited to sit down. In every sitting room, however small, there are as many chairs as could possibly fit into the room, and the invitation to sit down is made immediately and at times quite demandingly if the guest, as in the case of a Swedish newcomer, does not understand that she should accept the invitation.

Conversation is also an important part of having cultura and validating oneself as a true Cuban. In a group of people, the conversations are often about daily events and mutual acquaintances, activities such as weddings, or, of course, what there is to buy where. Being able to tell jokes and being amusing are also important parts of being a fully social person (cf. Gilmore 1980:114). Being quiet is seen as somewhat threatening, and people who say little are urged to talk and asked what is wrong and why they do not say anything. A television is almost always on in all houses, and if it is off when a visitor comes, it is put on and acts as a sound wall to the conversation. If there is something very interesting on the screen or the conversation falters, the events on the screen become welcome topics for continued conversation.

Cultura is built on giving and receiving. Guests receive total attention but are also expected to be entertaining and, above all, to open their homes just as generously.

One organized way to show generosity and hospitality is to throw a party. There are some events that should be celebrated, such as the first birthday of a child, *los quinze* (the fifteenth birthday of a girl), and weddings. Such parties almost always have a fixed form, although they might seem completely chaotic to an outsider. Their most important features are the photography and the food and drink.

Weeks before Suleyda's one-year birthday party, Popi, the father of the little girl, invited me. He reminded me of the party every time I met him after that. It was going to be on the afternoon of her birthday, which fell on a work-free Saturday, at the home of the young family who lives with the father of the wife. I went with a neighbor and her little son. We were told to arrive at 2:00, and at 2:30 we set off.

When we arrived, some other guests were already present and the place was chaotic. The women who were preparing the rice and beans and tubers and making the decorations, were still in hair rollers and work clothes, while the men, shirtless, were roasting a pig over an open fire and making a goat fricassee. Every now and then they cooled themselves with beers taken from a plastic container filled with ice. Children were running and playing all over the place. Popi and his wife, Tania, came to greet me and my friend and gave us each a beer. The son of my neighbor gave a little present to Suleyda, and I gave a bottle of rum to Popi. We sat down and talked on chairs that the hosts had carried out onto the patio, while the host family was running around making last-minute preparations. At 4:00, more guests arrived. The family emerged newly showered and in their party clothes. The photographer and some of Popi's relatives, who were coming from another place in Palmera, had not arrived yet. Everyone was drinking, talking, and joking, and the atmosphere was very relaxed. When Popi's relatives arrived, his brother brought a huge casette recorder and tapes, and soon music blared all over the neighborhood.

Now it was really a party. People had to shout to make themselves heard, but they didn't mind. Some danced, and the rum was brought out. Then the photographer, who was also a friend of the family, came, and all activities stopped as Popi urged everyone to go to a neighbor's house, where the cake was being kept, to be photographed. The cake, which was pink since the party was for a girl, was enormous and mounted on a table decorated with little boxes of candy and bottles of soft drinks. The birthday girl was put behind the table, while her small friends gathered around. First the girls, then the boys, and then different sets of adult friends and relatives all had to be photographed.

When the photo session was finished, everyone trotted up to the house again as Popi and his father carried the cake. Now it was dark and the patio was lit with one single light bulb hung in a tree. The women of the family went into the house, where the men had brought the pig and the goat fricassee, and for each person, they filled two little brown paper boxes of a type that is always used at parties, one with the hearty food, the other with a piece of cake, some *ensalada fría* (a macaroni salad with mayonnaise), and sweets. Meanwhile, Tania gave out presents—books, paper masks, paper hats, and some small toys—to all the children. A piñata, filled with sweets and small toys, was suspended above the children and then broken so that all the items fell out. The children threw themselves on the ground and fought for the bits and pieces. The bigger children could hoard more things, and the little ones cried. A big girl gave some candy to one of the little boys, who walked away happy.

The boxes containing the food and cake were passed around first to the children, who also got soft drinks, and then to the grown-ups. People ate with their hands or with a piece torn from the box. During all this time Popi and Tania passed around beer and rum, urging people to drink and asking if they were having a good time. People were becoming a little tipsy. They danced and talked, and everyone was given boxes of food to take home for those who could not come to the party. The night was cool and all of us were enjoying ourselves. When my neighbor and I left at 11:30, people were still dancing and drinking.

This was a lavish party with lots of gifts for the children and lots of food and drink. Weddings and fifteenth-year parties are similar, except that there are no children's gifts or piñata. Many parties are much simpler than Popi's, for although he does not earn much money, he has many relatives and a job that takes him around the municipality so that he can obtain a lot of things. Hosting a grand party might also be more important to him because he does not have a prestigious position in society. Parties can be a way of repaying gifts or help received or seen as investments for assistance needed later.

People also like to throw parties spontaneously when they have the means. Especially in the summertime, many a pig, a cherished party food, is roasted out of doors, at a beach, or on a riverbank. Then people eat, drink beer and rum, and immerse themselves in the cool water, making conversation, joking, and laughing. Since food is scarce and it is difficult to get hold of what is needed beyond rationed foodstuffs, one has to have access to a farmer who can sell a pig or raise one oneself in a back yard.

People do not go to parties uninvited because it is so difficult to get food and drinks, and, as a friend explained, it would be a terrible embarrassment for the host if there was not enough for everyone to eat, or, preferably, more than enough. Having more than people can drink is virtually impossible, so that the number of crates of beer available at a party is a valid measurement of its success.

Following the rules of social reciprocity is a way of showing one is a good Cuban, a socially competent and acceptable person. It is also a way of creating and maintaining social relations. A person who cannot or does not want to act according to these rules is excluded from enjoying many social relations. With relatives, reciprocity is important in maintaining the relationship. With friends, reciprocity is necessary to have a relationship at all.

Social relations not only are extremely important as emotional outlets in Cuba but are imperative for the survival of the Cuban people, since the social dimension of reciprocity is intimately linked to and necessary for the economic dimension of reciprocity to continue.

[3]

Men and Women in Palmera

During a recess in a meeting of the municipal Federación de Mujeres Cubanas, I stood talking and joking with Pedro, Carlos, Muñoz, and José in the shadow of a big tree in front of the cinema in Limones, where the meeting was being held. Alina, a young woman from Palmera, had made a rather radical speech earlier in the meeting about the importance of not accepting men's refusals to help with chores at home and with the upbringing of children. In fact, she said, we should not talk about *help*; men should do half the work, and we should not *ask* but tell them to do it.

At least one of the men, all of whom were leaders, or had political posts in Palmera, had talked during the meeting about the need for equality between men and women and the importance of the family in bringing up both boys and girls to have more egalitarian attitudes. During the recess, however, the men made sarcastic comments about the "feminist"[1] speech and implied that they certainly did not have the time to do housework, nor did they feel like doing it. That was their wives' job. "And by the way," said Pedro, "I wash dishes like a horse." I answered: "I know that, I have never seen a horse wash dishes." The men shook their heads, laughed, and said, as they always did when I caught on to a Cubanism, "Oh, Mona, you know too much." But the implication was

[1]This is my wording. The women in Palmera never used the term *feminism* and according to Marvin Leiner (1994:75), the FMC does not use the term either, since it is associated with capitalist societies that have not undergone revolutions.

clear: Pedro would not wash dishes or do anything else in the house if he could help it.

After more laughs and some coarse jokes, the men touched on what they seemed to feel was the real issue: Alina wanted all men to become like her husband. She had certainly forced him to do housework, "and look at him . . . ," they said, strongly implying that he was more effeminate than was good for him. They laughed uproariously. "You would never catch me with an apron, washing on the balcony," said José. "We are born different," added Carlos. "Women don't have mustaches, for example, so why should we do the same things?" The others agreed emphatically.

This scene illustrates many of the ambiguities of gender relations in Palmera. Men and women formally have equal rights in most areas. Women have their own organization, La Federación de Mujeres Cubanas, which nationally is very radical in its views. Many women have jobs outside the home and take part in military training, and some also hold political office. Women can and do speak up for themselves, and there are laws and regulations that stipulate their rights. The laws and regulations are not always followed, however (Bengelsdorf 1988; Rosenthal 1992), and, more important, traditional attitudes regarding gender issues are still prevalent among both men and women, which makes gender equality rather limited in everyday life. In reality, there is both gender stratification and a gendered division of labor (see Saltzman Chafetz 1991). Men have most of the power in Cuban society, both as political leaders and by virtue of their having the top positions in state companies and organizations. Women are supposed to exercise the quadruple roles of mother, housekeeper, wife/lover, and worker, an order of importance most men and many women would agree with, although some would also add revolutionary as a primary and all-inclusive role.

The ideas that the men outside the FMC meeting expressed are closely related to the gender ideal of machismo, which is widespread throughout Cuba and all Latin countries. Machismo suggests an exaggerated display of manliness[2] but also the idea that men should

[2]For definitions of machismo, see, for example, Bohman 1984; Gilmore 1990:4, 99, 167; Gilmore and Gilmore 1979; Gissi Bustos 1976; Lancaster 1992; Latin American and Caribbean Women's Collective 1977; Leiner 1994.

have supremacy and control over women in every aspect of life and that both physically and psychologically, men and women are in different spheres. Machismo is also, as Leiner (1994:79) says and as this and the following chapters shall make clear, "a particular form of patriarchy that has as much to do with public relations between men as between men and women."

The men no doubt were showing off to me and to each other, proving what real men they were and teasing me, because they knew that I agreed with Alina's ideas. Still, the rejection of anything that is not seen as manly is very common. Noteworthy in this particular case, one of the men was a close friend of Alina's husband, and one of the others was rumored to be bisexual. This did not, however, stop these men from going along with the jokes. The ideas that Alina advocated were very radical in Palmera, and many of the women certainly flinched at her militant way of expressing them. Yet many women agreed with the gist of what she was saying. The men felt irritated, and maybe also threatened by her speech, and resorted to coarse joking to take the edge off her criticism.

The gender system in Palmera, as in most parts of Cuba, is based on an inheritance of Mediterranean and Caribbean views of gender. The emphasis is on honor and shame, although these words are seldom used. Virginity, motherhood, and chastity are important female traits, while the male is seen as the protector of and provider for his family, as well as a virile lover. The more Caribbean traits of open eroticism and matrifocality and the frequent shifting of partners are also common. Since Palmera is a predominantly rural area where until recently people lived rather isolated lives, many people behave as they did before the revolution. In Havana and other bigger cities, however, many men and women with higher education no longer idealize the more blatant forms of machismo.

As I shall discuss in the following chapters, much of Cuba's socialist ideology is actively spread to everyone and accepted by many people. In the area of gender relations, however, the ideological messages of equality that the FMC and the Party have conveyed have been almost totally lost on the men in Palmera, as well as on many of the women. It is not only the less politically interested, or people with a "low" *nivel* (cultural and educational level), who accept and act out the ideas of machismo (cf. Leiner 1994:75), although more educated men at least verbally agree that men and women should be equal. The men who were joking during the recess of the FMC meeting would all adhere to the ideal of *plena igualdad* (total equality), but they do not live accordingly. As they said, they would not do housework, and like most other men in Palmera, they live "on the street" and have one, two, or more mistresses. Most men in Palmera would probably define equality in social structural terms, meaning they would say that women have a high level of equality already since they can work outside the home, get an education, and take part in politics, while many women complain about such everyday realities as their having total responsibility for the housework and the children. As I shall show, there are discrepancies not only between the ideals of *plena igualdad* and the ideas of machismo but also between ideals and practice in the realm of gender. Some of these discrepancies can be explained by gender division, while others are founded on diverse attitudes and experiences among women and among men.

Changes in the Lives of Women

Great changes have occurred in the lives of both men and women in Cuba since the revolution, but women have certainly experienced the greatest changes (cf. Bengelsdorf 1988; Casal 1980; Leiner 1994; Murray 1979). Before the revolution few women worked outside the home (Larguia and Dumoulin 1985; Leahy 1986; Moore 1988; Ravenet Ramirez, Pérez Rojas, and Toledo Fraga 1989). In 1953, for example, only about 10 percent of all women were working in the waged sector. Of those women who worked then, 30 percent were domestic servants (Casal 1980:191). Prostitution also was widespread. The differences between classes and between rural and urban areas were enormous. Although upper-class women in Havana in the beginning of the twentieth century had already formed feminist organizations[3] (see Stoner 1991), many women in rural areas like Palmera were virtually the property of first their fathers and brothers and later

[3]These women's organizations supported women as mothers and wives but usually did not challenge the patriarchal structure of the society.

their husbands. The women worked hard on the family farm until they got married. They got very little education, and many women (and men) who today are forty or fifty years old or older have had only a few years of schooling.

Today some 40 percent of the workforce in Cuba is female (Ravenet Ramirez, Pérez Rojas, and Toledo Fraga 1989:26; Smith and Padula 1988). Many of them—23 percent of all female workers—work in education (Ravenet Ramirez, Pérez Rojas, and Toledo Fraga 1989:31). Women are exempt from labor in the most heavy and dirty jobs, but otherwise they work in all sectors, although only 6 percent are in administration and 9 percent in agriculture (ibid.:33). Of the total female workforce in Palmera, however, as much as 29 percent are in agriculture, 23 percent in education, and 15 percent in health care and sports.[4] Women get eighteen weeks' leave from work six weeks before and 12 weeks after delivery, and can be moved to easier or less dangerous work during pregnancy (Randall 1981; Ravenet Ramirez, Pérez Rojas, and Toledo Fraga 1989; Stone 1981:134).

The Family Code, a law adopted in 1975, states that men and women must work together in the home, that children born out of and inside wedlock have equal rights, that parents must bring up their children together in a socialist spirit, and that both partners in a marriage have equal rights and duties (Ravenet Ramirez, Pérez Rojas and Toledo Fraga 1989:29; Stone 1981:appendix B).

There is no doubt that the women of Cuba have advanced enormously in social and economic position. Political leaders have reached their goals in many respects, but there is still a long way to the plena igualdad that the Women's Federation of Cuba advocates.

Marriage and Family

When Palmerans talk about *familia*, they mean various things (cf. Jelin 1991a). They may mean the nuclear family, which is the modern ideal; they may mean their relatives—parents, siblings, aunts, uncles,

[4]The figures, from 1989, come from the statistical unit of the Poder Popular in Palmera.

cousins; or they may mean their household, which usually includes some extended family.

Most commonly, the household consists of a mother, a father or other man who is living with the mother, married children, and their spouses and children. This is because of the housing shortage throughout Cuba. Relatives such as an unmarried uncle, a divorced brother or sister, or an elderly parent who must leave his or her house for one reason or another might also live with the family. According to both themselves and others, single men especially need to live with relatives, since they do not cook, wash their clothes, or clean house.

Most people feel that it is their duty to take care of their parents when they get old, and although the parents may not live with a child, they often visit and stay for a while. If the parents or relatives are sick, often a female relative will stay with the sick person to help. People seem to regard at least the siblings and parents of a couple as immediate family and feel that the couple has obligations toward them. Each member of the family is expected to help the others.

The composition of the household changes often, because most men and women change partners several times during their lives and thus have several different sets of children. There is a matrifocal orientation in Palmera, in that many women live for some time of their lives with their different sets of children and with their mother and/or sisters. Most of the time, however, a woman lives with some man. When a woman meets a new man, they move in together, she brings her children into the new family, and he may bring some of his children or some relative to the house.[5]

Many couples today live in common-law marriages, which have long been a tradition in Palmera. There were few priests and churches in Palmera before the revolution and people lived scattered in the mountains, so they just moved in together and were then regarded as married. Still, all couples in Palmera use the word for

[5]The Brazilian barrio that Claudia Fonseca (1991) studied exhibited similar traits—frequent changes in partners, the men's life in the street, and their autonomy—but when couples form a new union, they move to a new house and the woman may be obliged to leave her children by other men to relatives.

marrying legally, *casarse*, and women call their husbands *marido* (husband), whether they are legally married or not (cf. Smith 1988). The old custom of *llevarse* (eloping) is still practiced by some couples (cf. Martínez Alier 1972). Typically, the man takes the woman to a place where they spend the night and have sexual intercourse, which is the official beginning of the common-law marriage. This may be done secretly if the man and woman think that their parents will not approve. Otherwise, the man tells his future parents-in-law that he will llevarse the girl to his house or some other place.

The importance of the family as the basic and stabilizing unit in society was discussed in the political organizations during my fieldwork in Palmera (cf. Bengelsdorf 1988). The Party and the Women's Federation in Palmera encourage people to marry legally. They talk about the upbringing of the children as the task of both the mother and the father, and they stress the legal protection for women and children within marriage. Actually, a woman has legal rights when she has lived with a man in common law marriage for a certain period. The Party and the FMC seem to think that legal marriage will keep the unions more stable and slow down the rate of "divorces" and changes in partners. This has not proved true yet, and separations and divorces continue to be common. International missions and work mobilizations in other areas, which take people from their homes, are sometimes disruptive to relationships. In addition, young professionals have to do social service for two or more years after finishing school, often far from home. Many of these young people have children and are married, but when they go away they very often meet another partner and the marriage breaks up.

The Women's Federation sometimes organizes *bodas colectivas* (collective weddings) in an area. Then couples who have lived together for five, ten, or even twenty-five years may marry along with "new" couples. At a collective wedding I attended in Limones, there were nine couples and the oldest couple had lived together for fifteen years. Two couples were young and had never lived together. All the couples went to the marriage registration office and were married together, but afterward each couple had its own party. The Women's Federation helped organize the weddings and also provided beer and cakes. Some of the couples seemed to have been carried away by the idea of having a party, for after only eight to nine months, two of them had separated.

The Women's Federation also tries to prevent very young girls from marrying or moving in with their boyfriends and having children. It is not unusual to see girls of fifteen or sixteen with babies (cf. Leiner 1994; Rosenthal 1992; Smith 1992). The Women's Federation emphasizes that such girls are not adult enough to take care of children properly and that they have to discontinue their education when they become pregnant. These social realities run counter to the wish for female emancipation that the FMC works for. But as in other aspects of life, traditions are difficult to break.

Gloria told me proudly that her thirteen-year-old son, had many *novias* (girlfriends). She also said that if his girl had a child while both the youngsters were still in school, she would stay home from work and take care of it. She did not seem to see any problem with this.

The Street and the House

The classical division of public and private spheres as universal dichotomies (Rosaldo and Lamphere 1974) has been much criticized in anthropological and feminist writing (cf. Bohman 1984; di Leonardo 1991; Leahy 1986:94). In Palmera, however, "the street" and "the house" are emic concepts that imply different gender ideals and an ideal gendered division of the lives of men and women. Although men and women meet at home and in workplaces, do political work together, and have love affairs, attitudes in support of gender division are still strong, and both men and women defer to these norms. Even Alina who spoke out at the FMC meeting on equality within the home, would not and does not demand such equality in her own house, in spite of what the men were saying.

The men's sphere ideally is *en la calle* which means out in public, in official life. Describing a similar situation in Spain, David Gilmore (1990) says that men are even forced out into "the street" so as not to be considered unmanly. Men are expected to support their families by working outside the home, ideally in responsible and manly jobs. Most men in Palmera work in agriculture (56 percent of the male workforce).[6] It is not prestigious work, but it is often laborious and is seen as manly. The next biggest concentration of men—9 percent—work in construction, which is also viewed as tough and manly labor. Being a chauffeur also is a highly desired and prestigious job among men.[7] Chauffeurs learn to drive and repair cars, scarce resources in Cuba, and they meet many people and can develop new relationships, which is also a very important part of a man's life. Most men come home at night tired from their work and are served by the women of their family. They read the paper or watch television while they wait for dinner. They also spend much time with friends and acquaintances, drinking, playing dominoes, and chasing women. They go to parties alone and enjoy themselves with other women, dancing, drinking, and joking.

The women's sphere is in the house. This ideal has not changed, although many women in Palmera today also work outside the house. Kristina Bohman (1984) has pointed out that, even for housewives, the fact that a woman belongs *en la casa* does not mean that she is confined to the house. Nonetheless, the phrase symbolizes and connects womanhood, housework, and motherhood. In Palmera today, the house retains this symbolic meaning. Women must show that they "belong" to the house, their husband, and their children, although they might also hold demanding full-time jobs outside the home. This "belonging" is expressed mainly in the women's deferent attitudes toward men and in their not being "bossy" or "vulgar." Women in Palmera ideally should have their center of gravity in the house and not "run around in the streets" or to official places alone. One often sees women traveling or walking around with their own or other children as "chaperones." A "good" woman stays in the house as much as possible and leaves only when she has errands to do. She works hard, cleaning, cooking, washing clothes, and ironing.

Like most women in other parts of the world who work full time outside the home, Cuban women indeed have double burdens. Anita is a teacher who lives with her husband and her two children. Her husband and her young daughter occasionally help her in the home.

[6]This figure, from 1989, comes from the Statistical Unit of the Poder Popular in Palmera.

[7]Tony Larry Whitehead (1986:215) makes the same observation for Jamaica.

Sometimes her husband and daughter wash the dishes, her daughter often mops the floors, and her husband sometimes heats food or even fries meat, but Anita does most of the housework and definitely shoulders responsibility for it.

Anita gets up at 5:30 in the morning and starts preparing the food for lunch. She cleans and rinses the rice, fries meat, and prepares the viandas. She then makes breakfast for the rest of the family, usually milk and coffee and bread. Her husband and children eat and then go to work and school. Anita starts work at 7:50 A.M. but lives very close to her job, so she leaves the house at about 7:40. She teaches until 12.30 P.M., when the lunch break starts. Anita goes home to heat up the food she made in the morning, and she and her daughter set the table and serve the food to her husband and son. After everyone has eaten, Anita puts away the plates and cutlery and washes the dishes. She tidies up a bit in the kitchen, and if she has time, she rests in front of the TV.

At 1.30 P.M. Anita goes back to school, and the rest of the family also leaves the house. Back at school, Anita works by herself until 2.30, when her pupils join her for a couple of hours of mostly non-intellectual activities, such as working in the garden, sports, or music. From 4.20 P.M. to 5:00, Anita works alone again, doing administrative work or preparing for the next day. She then goes home. She might stop on her way to see if there are any vegetables or *viandas* at the parallel market or other items to buy in the supermarket.

When Anita arrives home she starts to prepare dinner and cleans up a little, sweeping the floors if not mopping them, ironing, or preparing for the next day. Before dinner, she and the whole family shower, sometimes in water she heats. After dinner, she washes the dishes and tidies the kitchen. At about 8:00 she can sit down for a while in front of the television or chat with a visitor. Approximately every second week she has a meeting of some kind in the evening, of the CDR, FMC, or the union.

Every second week Anita also works on Saturday.[8] When she is free on Saturday, she uses that day to wash clothes for the family. She has a Soviet-made washing machine that she has to fill with water by hand and later she must also rinse the clothes by hand, but at

[8]Every second week all Cubans work full days on Saturdays.

least the machine washes the clothes. She hangs the clothes on the balcony. With the help of her daughter, she also cleans the house. She sweeps the floors and then washes them, using at least two changes of water.

On Sunday Anita irons the clothes, which are now dry, and does some other chores in the house. Often she must prepare classes for school since she has so little time during the week. One Sunday each month, on la Día de la Defensa (Defense Day), Anita goes to military training. When she is free on both Saturday and Sunday, she relaxes with her family on at least one of those days. Sometimes they visit a relative or a friend or go to the beach, and at least she can sleep a few hours after lunch. Otherwise her days are full of work, like those of most women in Palmera (cf. Ravenet Ramirez, Pérez Rojas, and Toledo Fraga 1989). During the afternoon, before her husband comes home, Anita might see her female neighbors, but not for long and preferably when they are out on some errand. A Palmeran woman does not generally invite a male visitor in the house when she is alone. If she does, the door is often left open so that anyone can see into the house or enter without trouble, assuring everyone that nothing "fishy" is going on. Anita spends most of her waking hours at work, which she loves. Doing a good job is vital to her. Yet, as a woman, she is defined by her roles in the home, as the wife of Papito, the mother of her two children, and the mistress of the house.

The Ideal Man and Woman

The most important role officially advocated for men and women in Cuba is that of revolutionary. Both men and women are expected to sacrifice all for society and the revolution. Nonetheless, there are different gender ideals. Men and women are seen as very different in their abilities and their personalities.

Un verdadero hombre (a real man) in Palmera is one who provides for and protects his family (Gilmore 1990). He is expected to *cargar a la casa* (literally, carry to the house)—that is, to support his family and care for their well-being—although in many families the woman earns as much as or more than the man. A good man in Palmera also looks for food to buy whenever he goes to other towns or villages, and sometimes he buys the monthly rationed goods and carries them home.

Palmeran men generally do very little housework. They make small repairs and take out the garbage, and often they do this at night so as not to be seen.

A real man in Palmera is brave and takes initiatives, and he is autonomous. Most Palmeran men do not account for their whereabouts when they leave the house, and they consider it irritating if they are asked where they have been when they return home. Men are also expected to protect the honor of their women and children by controlling their behavior outside the home. Today this is difficult, and if a man's wife or daughters behave dishonorably in public, it reflects badly on him. A real man is also a very social person who likes to drink, to go to parties, to converse, and to be generous with himself and his time and money. He should be able to tell jokes and stories and to sing and dance well. Most men like to dress well and are well groomed. Many men who work in offices change their shirts twice a day to look cool and clean. They wear short-sleeved shirts and trousers or blue jeans to work or for leisure and guayabera, the traditional Cuban shirt with pleats, when they want to look more formal. The only time I saw a man wear a suit in Palmera was when he got married. At home, men often wear thin trousers or shorts and go bare-chested when only the family is present. They keep their hair cut short.[9]

Being a real man also involves being strong, a trait that is often demonstrated by carrying heavy burdens with apparent ease, working extremely hard in bouts, and occasionally fighting with other men, although that shows a certain lack of cultura. For a man in Palmera, nothing is more damaging to his *hombría* (manliness) than showing weakness. He must definitely not be effeminate in any way, which might be signaled by talking in an unusually high-pitched voice or doing housework in the sight of others (cf. Leiner 1994).

The homophobia is overt (cf. Arguelles and Rich 1984) in Cuban society. The state denies known homosexuals some types of jobs and access to Party membership (cf. Randall 1981).[10] It is a terrible

[9]In 1995, I saw many younger men in Havana with long hair and ponytails.

[10]The film *Fresa y Chocolate* (*Strawberry and Chocolate*), made by Tomás Alea

offense for a man to be accused of being a *pájaro* or *maricón* (a homosexual), and calling someone a *maricón* is a terrible insult. As in most places in the world, there are homosexuals in Palmera, but most are married and live out their homosexuality in extreme secrecy. Even the suspicion of being homosexual is stigmatizing. A woman told me that she had divorced her husband because she thought he was a homosexual. She had never dared ask him, but others had told her, and he had many friends who were said to be homosexuals. She had lived for many years regretting that she divorced him based on suspicions and gossip, because she liked him a lot. Many parents also voice concerns that their sons are pájaros if they do not have enough girlfriends when they are eleven or twelve years old, and they encourage boys to go out en la calle at a young age.

The worst affront a man can experience is that his woman *le pega tarros* (puts horns on him) by being unfaithful. This shows him to be weak, one of the most shameful experiences for a man, and that he cannot control his wife. It might also reflect on his sexual abilities, an even bigger disgrace. Both men and women regard a man who has "horns" as somewhat ridiculous. A man in Palmera whose wife, it was said, was repeatedly unfaithful to him with different men went back to her after having moved out for a while. In many people's eyes, this made him truly despicable. A female friend of mine saw him at the beach and said, "Look at that white frog; isn't he pitiful!" It seemed that he was more stigmatized for accepting her behavior than she was in being unfaithful. Not so long ago, male Party members who could not "control" their unfaithful wives were expelled from the Party.

The "real" man in Palmera has more than one woman at a time, *la otra* (the other woman) being a common concept in Palmera. But he must engage in his adventures discreetly, so as not to embarrass his family more than necessary.

Gutiérrez and Juan Carlos Tabío and released in 1993, gives an illuminating view of a homosexual's life in Cuba, based on a prize-winning essay and later a book, *El Lobo, el Bosque y el Hombre Nuevo* (1994), by Senel Páz. That it was shown extensively in Cuba indicates that the official view of homosexuality is changing, although there do not seem to have been any real changes in daily life.

When talking about men en la calle, Alicia, a middle-aged office worker, told me and some other women that her father was a real womanizer. He always had other women, and she knew of some half-brothers and half-sisters, but she said with pride, "He always handled it discreetly, and my mother never knew anything about it." The other women seemed skeptical that she did not know—"women know these things," as they often say—but they also seemed to agree that, since it was inevitable, it was good that the man respected his wife and did not go around showing off his other women. The women also say that an intelligent woman should never mention that she knows that her husband has a lover or two, and definitely not that she knows who they are. Sometimes one learns of arrangements in Palmera that amount to polygyny: a man who has two houses and two sets of women and children that he supports.

Men in Palmera seem to seek a balance (Whitehead 1986) between what Peter Wilson (1973) calls respectability and reputation.[11] A man's respectability is upheld principally through his being the protector of and provider for his family, thereby emphasizing his roles as husband, father, and relative. His reputation is upheld through his role as lover, womanizer, and "chum." When a man has a new woman, he does not flaunt her in front of everyone. The news about the new woman, however, always "leaks out" to others. If he is too discreet, so that no one knows about his adventures, he might risk being considered less manly. He can be too much of a womanizer, however, especially if he is careless and does not protect his family from the knowledge of his affairs. He is then called a *zorro* (literally, a fox) and loses his respectability in the eyes of women and perhaps also of other men.

A man is expected to respect his wife by being discreet in his womanizing but also by being courteous and considerate. Standing on my balcony one evening, Graciela and I saw García come out of his house with his wife and young son. They went to their car, and the wife got into the back seat, while the son joined his father in front. "There you have a real zorro," Graciela said. "He is sleeping

[11]Contrary to Wilson's account, in Cuba respectability does not have anything to do directly with class but is expected in everyone.

around everywhere. And look, she has to sit in the back of the car! That is *falta de respeto* [disrespectful]. García should tell that kid of his to move and let her sit in front. Show some respect!" Graciela was obviously upset that this man was behaving so badly toward his wife.

A good woman in Palmera is almost the opposite of a good man. Her most valued roles are those of mother and wife. Motherhood is almost sacred, and both men and women talk about their mothers as the most important people in their lives. On Mother's Day, which is celebrated extensively in Palmera, everyone brings gifts to his or her mother or leaves flowers at the cemetery if the mother is dead. Women often send greeting cards to each other on Mother's Day. Even I and other women who did not have children but were of the "right" age received cards.

As a mother, a woman has a high status, and very few women would consider not having children voluntarily. Most women say that their children are their lives. When talking about her only son, Irina once told me: "Ah, Mona, now I think a lot about when Carlito will move away from home. Then I will be *solita, solita* (completely alone)." That she would still be living with her husband somehow did not count (cf. Ravenet Ramirez, Pérez Rojas, and Toledo Fraga 1989: 147). Other women expressed the same sadness about the time when their children would leave home.

Thus, the Cuban woman, like other socialist women, is a "working-mother," as Maxine Molyneux (1981:21) has put it. She feels her own and others' demands to be a good mother and housewife, a good worker, and, at least in Cuba, a good revolutionary. As Molyneux also points out, the emblem of the FMC is "a woman with a gun in one hand and a baby in the other" (ibid:21).

A woman is also expected to be a good wife, faithful, sacrificing, and tolerant. In talking about her sick husband, Gloria explained her view of womanhood:

> Well, I tell you, I have never thought about leaving him. Do you know why? Because my deceased mother said that when a woman marries a man she has to die with this man. She should die with this man, and even more so if this man is good. When I married she said that she

> had lived with my dad for thirty years and that I should be like her. It is not an obligation, but it is a recommendation from my mother. And now when Antonio is sick, I cannot leave him even if I get ideas sometimes to leave him and go. I mustn't, I mustn't. One should *cumplir* [honor the vow] to the end. If a woman marries a man she should . . . and he too, if he marries a woman, should take care of his wife. To the end. Even if he falls in love en la calle. What the woman must not do is fall in love in the street, but the man, well, he does not have more right but . . . the woman ought to respect the man. The man should respect the woman also, but well, they fall in love, you know how it is in the street.

"What do you think of that?" I asked.

"Well, chica, it's normal, that gusto is normal, that they fall in love en la calle, well, you know. The man is a man" (cf. Ravenet Ramirez, Pérez Rojas, and Toledo Fraga 1989:104).

Most women in Palmera agree that men fall in love more easily than women, have insatiable sexual lust, and must be allowed to have various women, even if the women feel bad about being betrayed. Most men seek a good housekeeper and presumtive mother to marry and then have las otras as stimulating sex partners and companions.

Women should be attractive, wives moderately so, so as to represent the family honorably. Palmeran women wear sexy, clingy slacks to show off their bottoms, which are considered the most sexy part of the body—the bigger the better. The most popular slacks are of an elastic cloth, in gaudy colors, and are worn skin tight. These slacks are considered "good" ones, to be worn at work or when going out. Women also wear low-cut or see-through blouses, costume jewelry, and high heels, but never to the extent of being tarty. When Palmeran women want to really dress up, they wear dresses or a blouse and skirt of some shiny cloth in a low-cut, sleeveless style with closed shoes or pumps, in a matching color. At home women often wear loose shifts of some thin and cool material or shorts, but they would never leave the house in such clothes. They wear makeup when going out and tint their hair and set it often. If they do not have time to fix their hair, they put on rollers and a scarf, which are considered acceptable to wear in public. They go to the manicurist often, and most women have long, painted nails.

Almost from birth boys and girls in Palmera are brought up differently. In my barrio a group of boys was always playing ball and running around shouting in the street at night. They stayed out until late and their mothers sometimes shouted at them to come in, but usually they were left alone. Boys are expected to and are allowed to do more than girls. They are brought up to be manly, not to cry, and to be aggressive in their relations with other boys, but also to be gallant and polite to grown-ups and girls. By the time they are ten or eleven years old, they are supposed to have "girlfriends," and parents and other grown-ups ask and joke about them. Boys also have fewer tasks in the house, and when they are asked to buy the bread or to do some other chore, they usually can avoid it and will not be scolded much.

Girls, by contrast, are expected to remain in the house, to help their mothers, and to be calm and sweet. Girls are expected to be attractive and prettily dressed and not to play roughly. A girl is not allowed to be out on the streets until she is quite old. Girls often go with their mothers when they leave the house and are accustomed to helping their mothers a lot with housework. This difference between boys and girls can be summed up in a word used by people in Palmera. The word *bandolera* is used about girls, and sometimes even women, who are seen to be too adventurous, to be out in the streets to much, to be too flirtatious or not modest enough. The word is hardly ever used in the masculine form.

Many people still feel that girls should be virgins until they get married (cf. Leiner 1994:81–84). At a wedding I attended, someone joked with the bride after the ceremony and said, "Here comes *Señora* Pérez!" The bride looked back at the person with apparent pride and said, "Señora no, todavía Señorita" (Mrs., no, still Miss) *Señorita* means both "Miss" and "virgin." She had not grown up in an especially traditional family, but she still seemed to feel that it was important to state that she had not yet lost her virginity. A man who takes the virginity of a girl incurs a more binding obligation toward her than toward other women. A woman told me that she had a lover who also had a relationship with a young girl. This young girl got pregnant, and since he had taken her virginity, he "had to marry her."

Eroticism and Jealousy

That something "fishy" must be going on when men and women meet in private is the common opinion of everyone in Palmera. A male friend of mine complained that men and women cannot meet in Palmera without people gossiping that they are having an affair. He mentioned that people were saying that about us but did not seem to mind very much. Another friend suggested that we go to bed, since everyone thought we were anyway.

Eroticism is ever-present in the life of Palmera. Men and women are always flirting, and it seems that every encounter is a probe into the possibilities of continuing the relationship. Both men and women constantly chase one another, and although most of the time this does not lead to a relationship, it is a way of enjoying oneself. Most men have a wife and maybe a lover and may not have time or the stamina for the new woman. But not to try when the opportunity comes along would be almost unthinkable and would seem unmanly. Some men certainly exaggerate the extent and number of their lovers, however, so as to enhance their reputations as manly.

Although both men and women appreciate the eroticism and sensuality, they have different views of it. Most men seem to enjoy the opportunities to have several women, while many women complain and see themselves at the losing end of the relationships.

Eduardo, a man in his early thirties, explained to me about love. Here in Cuba, he said, it is the men who *se enamoran* (fall in love). And when a man falls in love, he tells the woman, who is always reluctant. The man then constantly tries to convince her to begin a relationship; he talks to her, jokes with her, maybe gives her little presents, and visits her until she says yes. I asked if women did not fall in love. No, said Eduardo, they don't. But everyone does not accept or . . . ? I said suspiciously. Most of them do, Eduardo answered. After thinking for a while he continued, but, of course, there are those who say no all the time and then you have to accept that. You have to court various women at the same time, so if you are courting five or six, maybe two accept, he said. Eduardo was totally serious and said that this was not anything special to him but general for most men. He was probably right, even if a more sophisticated man would never have confessed so readily to adhering to such a pragmatic view of love affairs.

Women do not agree with this description. They say they fall in love and discuss strategies for "catching" a man. At these times all the ideals associated with being a woman are exaggerated, such as being beautiful, well dressed, modest, a good cook, moderately sexy, and not too eager. To show reluctance is said to enhance a man's interest. Women also describe men as very ardent and interested at the beginning of a relationship but also say, disappointedly, that when the man has "what he wants," namely, sex and a *compromiso* (agreement) from the woman, he often rapidly loses interest in her. It is the conquest that matters. The man may also lose interest because the ideal is that women should not "give in" too easily. Women may flirt but should not take initiatives toward sexual intercourse.

Both men and women agree that it is good for people to be married or to live together as a couple. This view is advocated partly because they believe no one should be alone. Among men, their homophobia might also contribute to their desire to show that everything is "all right" by living with a woman. Women get a secure social status by being married, whereas a single woman is seen as suspicious in many ways. Today few working women need to get married for economic reasons, but most women feel that it enhances their economic position. A friend of mine used to joke about looking for a man with PCC (which also is the abbreviation for the Party), namely, *Plata, Casa y Carro* (money, house, and a car). A good economic position is thus an advantage for a man, but it is by no means a necessity. Most women say that they want a "good" man or a "noble" man, which means a man who respects them and takes care of his family.

The logistics of the Palmerans' sexual relationships may seem complicated, but the constant change of partners makes it possible for men to have access to lovers all the time. There are, of course, men who do not have lovers, but when I asked people in Palmera if they could mention anyone, they usually thought for a long time and then said no or mentioned one name. There are a lot of divorces, which usually are caused by the man taking a lover. Subsequently, he leaves his wife and moves in with la otra, who then becomes the wife who must accept that her husband has other women. The divorced woman then becomes a possible otra or finds a man who is willing to divorce to marry her.

Graciela, a woman in her forties, told me about her life:

I tell you, I have been happy for a very short time in my life. I married my first husband in 1970. We were legally married, and after a year our son was born. We were living together with my father then, but I did not like that, so we got hold of this house and moved here when our son was six months old. I have lived here for eighteen years now, eighteen years. When my son was two years old I became pregnant again, but my husband was *de cabroncito* [sleeping around] then, always being *por la calle*, falling in love here and there, having women here and there. And I had an abortion. The first abortion I had was the last one, too; never again in my life.

Then things were bad for some years. He was still falling in love *en la calle.* I was always alone here. He worked in another town. At times he came home once a week; at times he did not come home at all. So I left him. And then I was pregnant again, so I went to the doctor to take it away. When I came there it was an old doctor and he checked me and said that he would not perform an abortion because I was too long gone. When he asked me how many children I had and I said one, he could not believe that I wanted to abort this one. So I did not do it, and it was a girl, Ingrid. We had some good years, my husband and I, and he loved me, but this stuff with the men in the street, it is an evil which always happens. Always. Some women suffer this in silence, but I would not do that. We lived together for eight years and then he went and married a woman in town. We got a divorce with papers, and he married la otra legally, too. He already had a daughter with her then. She is eleven now. When he had been married to her no more than a year, he fell in love with this one, that he has now. Because of that, the saying goes: He who loves, kills. My children suffered much, and I suffered much. I loved that man a lot.

One year after I got divorced, I met the man I later married [lived with]. I was having a very difficult time. I was alone and did not work and had to make a living for us three with thirty pesos [per month]. And nobody helped me. So I married him and we were together for eight years. He was not bad, but after a while he became a womanizer, too. We lived here a while separated, the two of us in the same house.

He refused to move out, but when he left he took everything we had—the TV, my sewing machine, the fridge, lots of things. But I did not want to have my children brought up with that. He threatened me, but I said, "You wouldn't dare," and he left. Now he lives in another place. We didn't have any children together. I do not want to have children with any other man. I do not want to have children with another surname[12] than the two I have.

Graciela's is a rather common fate for many women in Palmera. Most have been married or have lived in common-law marriages with several men during their life times. Many also have children with these men. Many women also had children when they were very young with men with whom they never lived. These children are usually welcomed, and there seem to be few problems between them and the man currently living in the household. These arrangements very much resemble the matrifocal households of some other Caribbean and African American communities (Smith 1988; Stack 1974).

Like Graciela, most younger Cuban women have had abortions, some as many as four. Sometimes the women have abortions instead of using contraceptives. If they get pregnant with a man with whom they do not want to live or when life is difficult, they get an abortion, which is free and available as long as there is no threat to the woman's life and she is less than twelve weeks' pregnant.

The reason given for divorces is almost always unfaithfulness on the part of the husband. Whether or not this leads to divorce depends on how much of his life en la calle the wife accepts and also on how discreet the man is. The divorces are often disruptive, and Graciela was lucky to be able to keep her house, although her husband took many of their possessions. Many couples cannot agree on who should have the house and therefore divide it in two parts. This has led to many people living in strange and cramped parts of houses with makeshift kitchens or bathrooms added on after the house was divided.

That Palmeran women almost always feel they are in competition

[12]Every person in Cuba has two surnames. The first one is the first surname of the father, and the second one is the first surname of the mother.

for men or in competition with other women leads to a shallow solidarity among women. There are otras who are said to call wives to tell them they are having relationships with their husbands, thereby hoping to start quarrels between the two.

One time when Vilma, Flora, and I were talking about men and unfaithfulness, Vilma said she could never take away the husband of a friend, while Flora was more uncertain and said that she thought she could if she really liked the man. She had done that once and it had led to a break between her and her friend, but she did not seem to think this was of any great consequence.

In spite of the potential for conflicts, lively and intense discussions about the problems of gender and machismo are carried on among female friends in Palmera. They freely complain that their husbands never help with the housework, and they discuss the need for child care. And, of course, they gossip about who has been seen with whom as well as the pros and cons of the men in the neighborhood. They talk about love and even discuss their own and their men's sexual behavior. They also agree that they feel insecure when their men are out en la calle with other women. They never know if their husband will leave them for la otra.

For both men and women, statements of jealousy are a means of claiming possession of the other in a relationship. A woman uses jealousy when she feels insecure to claim her right to be the only woman or at least the most important woman in her man's life. A man expresses jealousy out of a fear of having lost or of losing control over his woman.

Insofar as many men in Palmera lead very autonomous lives, the women often check up on their husbands, asking them where they have been when they come home late at night, although they know that they will never get a straight answer. They often quarrel and accuse their husbands of not doing enough around the house, of using it as a hotel, and so on. Sometimes they even stop talking to them or stop having sex with them. This can be a way of protesting what the women feel is unfair treatment, but it is also a form of erotic play and a way of affirming the relationship. The men very seldom move out on their own. Rather, their behavior provokes the women to throw them out. Many men have second thoughts when the woman finally does this and then want to come back. Men who feel rejected often take revenge by taking away all the items in the house that they have bought or helped buy.[13]

Palmeran men most often express their jealousy when they feel they are losing control. They often phrase their reproach in terms of honor: the woman has strayed too much from the house and they will not allow her to behave like a slut, to dishonor him and the family. But Palmeran men also like to control their women by commenting on and "forbidding" them to wear sexy clothes and to do things alone, without them.

One day when discussing men, Maribel said to Eva, who was living with a new man, "You say that you are so emancipated, but when Juan tells you not to wear tight shorts or not to smoke, you do as he tells you." Eva protested and said that this was not true, that she would never let a man decide what she should do, but as a matter of fact both Maribel and I had noticed a change in Eva. She often changed her ways so as to comply with Juan's wishes.

There seemed to be a constant tug of war between the men and women of Palmera over control. The women tried to stretch the limits of what was allowed, and the men tried to narrow them. The women often contradicted their husbands and did things they were not supposed to do. The man's protest then became a way of reestablishing his power, at least verbally. As long as the woman did not stray too far from the limits of how she was to behave, the bantering and mock quarreling seemed to be a form of lovemaking. When there were serious problems, men sometimes resorted to beating their women. At times this led to his killing the woman, and in most years there are one or two crimes of this type in Palmera.[14] Mostly the jealousy does not go this far but is expressed in quarrels or in the couple's splitting up. The man may move in with his mother or with another woman. Very often the couple gets together again after some time.

[13]This happened to Graciela and to many other women I knew in Palmera. Fonseca (1991) reports that she learned of the same behavior in a slum area of Brazil.

[14]Until 1930 there was an adultery law in Cuba, which meant that men who killed adulterous wives got very lenient or no punishment at all (see Stoner 1991:148–55).

The Women's Federation

The discourse on plena igualdad and the gender system is carried out principally by the Women's Federation. Although machismo is evident throughout Cuban society, its impact and interpretation and acceptance of it vary among different people and in different contexts. The contradictions in attitudes and variations in interpretations of the gender system among women are clearly visible in the different levels of the FMC.

When the FMC was introduced during the early part of the revolution, together with the Party, its role was to try to restructure Cuban society in line with the aims of the revolution. Women, it was said, should have the same rights and duties as men. Women took part in the literacy campaign, in defense and education, and in many other areas of society (Randall 1981; Ravenet Ramirez, Pérez Rojas, and Toledo Fraga 1989:23). Like other mass organizations, the FMC gained members throughout the country through base organizations in the barrios and villages. This meant that just about all women came into contact with the ideas and discussions of the FMC. It soon became both a moral and a political force, and women were urged to take part in the revolution as full members.

On the national level, the FMC today carries out a very radical discussion of machismo and the attitudes of men and women toward their gender roles (see Smith and Padula 1988). Its goal is to achieve total equality between men and women, but it also supports the Party and organizes women in voluntary work and the militia (cf. Leiner 1994:66).

On the municipal and local political levels, the FMC, together with the CDR monitors such antisocial behavior as wife beating and alcoholism, and disruptive children (see chapt. 6). It also urges women to take cytological tests[15] each year by making it one of the requirements for being a vanguard federada. The FMC is not regarded as a very important organization, however. Recruitment to its posts is often made haphazardly, and the most qualified women already have positions in the Party or the youth organization, which bring

[15]Since many women did not have themselves tested for cancer voluntarily, doctors developed a political means to get the tests done.

greater prestige. The FMC in Palmera does not function very well, although 82 percent of all women over the age of fourteen are members.[16] Some *delegaciones* (local base organizations) do a good job because they have efficient and enthusiastic members, but many others do little.

In my own FMC group, two housewives were the elected leaders, but they were not really interested in working with the organization. They had no experience with organizational work and were totally uninterested in learning. The two of them quarreled and eventually were not on speaking terms. This meant that the group functioned very badly. We had very few meetings, and those we had were just formal events held because they had to be held. We never discussed any women's issues related to our own experiences and never once touched upon the problem of machismo. A year after the group was constituted, there were no meetings and the delegación had no name. The leaders said that they had asked the municipal FMC to help because they did not know how to function better, but they had received no assistance. Other women made several suggestions to the leaders for improvements, but very little happened. When we eventually held a few meetings, no notes were taken and there were no agendas.

The ideas of the national FMC trickle down to the leaders at the municipal level, but these women often have very different life situations, which makes it difficult for the local women to accept the FMC's ideas completely. The local FMC in Palmera is also very close to the Party and therefore does not address gender issues that contradict those of the Party. At the discussions in Palmera leading to the Party Congress of 1991, several suggestions were made to merge the FMC with the CDR or to disband the FMC. Some felt that the FMC was not necessary anymore. Women had their equality and the FMC functioned badly, they said. Others felt that the close connection to the Party made the FMC play down the problems of women and function merely as an appendage to the Party. They suggested that the federation should be more independent.

The link between the Party and the FMC became very evident over the question of whether to build a day-care center in Limones.

[16]This figure was cited in an interview with the president of the FMC in Palmera.

There are no public child-care facilities in Palmera. To solve their child care needs, working women have to rely on their relatives or on other women who take care of children for a fee. For years, there have been discussions about building a day-care center in the town. Every now and then the question arises in political meetings. Women state that it is wasteful that they cannot work full time because of the difficulties with child care. The political leaders have claimed there was not enough money to do anything. They have also said there is no use in discussing the problem because there is no way of solving it. Privately many women express their bitterness and point out that there is money for many other things but that the need for a day-care center is seen as only a women's problem.

The municipal leaders of the FMC, try to spread the ideas that they feel are important. They visit the local delegaciones and send out material for discussions. Many of the radical ideas emanating from the national FMC seem foreign to the women in most of the base organizations, however. The gender issue most often discussed at the local level is how to get men to share in the responsibilities of home and children.

At an FMC meeting in a small village on the coast of Palmera, the women discussed a paper issued at the national level. The document emphasized the importance of bringing up boys and girls in the same way and of getting boys to help at home. It also stated that women had to demand of their men that they help more with the housework and care of the children. The women present, housewives and agricultural workers, giggled when the paper was read. They said that this was all very well and that men should help in the house and with the children. But they also said that they would never get their men to do this and that they thought it would take generations to change the men's behavior.

Although there is a big gap between the views of the leaders of the FMC and those of the grassroot members, there is obviously widespread interest in Palmera in matters of gender. This was evident at the municipal meeting of the FMC, where the discussions were lively and many women talked. They discussed the need for the day-care center, the education of women, and women in agricultural work and reinforced that both parents have to bring up children together. The president of the FMC said that was it a disgrace that many men still felt that it was the job of the mother to bring up the children. She produced laughter from the audience when she said that to this day there were men who said to their wives, "If she [their daughter] comes home pregnant, I'll kill you." The women agreed that all federadas must try to convince their husbands that they have to share this responsibility.

In the area of gender, the contradictions are both ideological and practical. Although the structural positions of men and women have changed enormously, old traditions and views are still prevalent. In Palmera plena igualdad is still mostly just an ideal, presented and articulated in official political contexts, such as the FMC meeting described above. Men frequently express skepticism about "feminist" ideas, while women generally seem to think that they are worth considering. When concrete ways of changing the gender system are mentioned many women are also skeptical. The ideas of machismo are strongly fixed in the life of Palmera although they are seldom articulated in official contexts. Some women want to challenge the machismo in practical action and want to try other ways of interacting, but the social control in this small municipality makes it very difficult to change the rules of gender relations.

Perhaps because most of the leaders of the revolution have been male, gender issues have not been high on the agenda. Even more important, as we shall see, the male gender ideal, embraced by both men and women, is an integral component of the ideal revolutionary.

[4]

The Soul of the Revolution

On a hot December afternoon I took part in the inauguration of a bridge on the Carretera Central, the main coastal highway in Palmera. The first secretary of the province, a huge black man, had arrived to cut the ribbon and to present gifts to those who had worked for more than twenty-five years on the road construction. The construction workers, wearing their work clothes and white hard hats, and the leaders of the municipality had already gathered on the bridge, where microphones were set up. On his arrival, the first secretary, who wore blue jeans and a white short-sleeved guayabera, quickly jumped out of his chauffeur-driven olive-green jeep and immediately walked up to the group of workers, greeted them, and started asking them how long the bridge was, how long it took to build, how much it cost, and other questions. The workers answered him readily and chatted amiably. This road had a highly symbolic value to the inhabitants and politicians of the region in that construction had been started after the revolution with the aim of making this formerly remote part of the province accessible to the rest of the country and linking the provinces on the southern coast with each other.

In his speech, the first secretary praised the revolution, which had made it possible to build the road, and he rattled off figures on the kilometers of road that had been built, the number of bridges that had been constructed, the tons of cement used and so on. He spoke without consulting notes, in the manner of Fidel. Each man was then called forward to receive his gift, a photo of the longest bridge on the highway, inscribed with his name and the names of the first secretaries of the province and municipality. The first secretary chatted with each of them. One worker, a chauffeur, had driven without having an accident for more than twenty-five years. He was very proud of this, and the first secretary congratulated and praised him for it. He showed his interest in the work the men had done and constantly emphasized the importance of their work for Cuban society and the revolution. When one of the workers, as black and as big as the first secretary, came up to receive his photo, the first secretary jokingly asked him if they were unknown brothers. The worker looked mischievous and answered that they might very well be. Everyone laughed. One of the men carried a poster that said "Group no. 5 promises to make the parts for the five bridges and the forty production units before the end of 1989," and the first secretary coaxed all of the men into promising that they would work longer hours and exert even more effort in the future. The men looked proud when they made their promise, and many of them talked about their gratitude to the revolution, saying that the road and the life they led would not have been possible without the revolution.

A worker was then called up to express the feelings of the Brigada (the work gang). He said that the workers had labored up to sixteen hours a day to finish the bridge. They made a promise to El Comendante en Jefe Fidel Castro to finish the road before the fourth Party congress, to be held in 1991. Everyone cheered. A young boy had been working with the construction workers on the bridge after school. He also received a gift, and the first secretary said that he was a good example to young people and adults alike and that it was spirit like his that helped make the revolution successful. He asked the boy to say something, but he was very embarrassed and did not know what to say. He stood for a while, shuffling his feet. Then the first secretary patted him on the back and said to everyone, "Well, some people don't say much, but they do so much more." Everyone smiled and applauded. When the meeting was over the workers came up to talk a bit more to the first secretary, who shooed away some reporters so he could talk to the workers.[1]

I witnessed many such ceremonies in Palmera during my field-

[1]For a comparison, see Lockwood 1990: chap. 1, which describes a meeting between the young Fidel Castro and some peasants in the Oriente.

work. This particular one illustrates, explicitly and implicitly, much of what will be discussed in this chapter, namely, the role of the Party and its cadres and the precarious balance between hierarchy/equality and centralism/participation inherent in Cuban politics.

At the bridge inauguration, the workers were shown appreciation not by being given higher salaries or better jobs but by being praised for their commitment to the revolution. The first secretary was a popular leader. The men knew him from television and newspapers, and some of them may had met him under similar circumstances before. Most people in the province admired his political shrewdness and knew that he had the ear of Fidel. He embodied the male ideals of strength, audacity, and enjoyment of life, which are also the ideals of a good leader. His imposing physique represented the male ideal of strength, and his tall and heavy frame and loud voice and laugh symbolized his role as provider and protector, while inspiring awe in those (leaders and other alike) whom he questioned and put in difficult spots when they did not accomplish their tasks. He emphazised his equality with the workers by wearing casual clothes and chatting and joking with them. He seemed genuinely to enjoy associating with the workers and made a point of addressing them and not talking to his fellow politicians. By joking that perhaps he and one of the workers were unknown brothers, he emphasized the theme of equality but also alluded to a common ideal—that of the virile man. He and other leaders also sometimes used a fatherly approach. He put his hand on workers' shoulders and acted in a very friendly manner. He encouraged and praised. Yet there was never any doubt who was the leader. He succeeded in impressing on the workers the importance of sacrifice for the cause of the revolution. He implied that they were all part of a larger mission, namely, to improve and perpetuate the revolution in Cuba. But they had different tasks, the workers', to construct with their hands, and the first secretary's abstractly and ideologically, to build the revolution.

By opening a dialogue with the workers, the leaders draw the workers into a conversation in which they open up about their experiences and are made to feel part of the struggle to produce a better society. They often formulate their responses in formalized ways, in slogans and rhetoric, but their experiences are theirs and are heard. Finally, the leaders exhort the people to work for the revolution, since ultimately talking is not enough, action is all that counts (see chap. 6).

Democratic Centralism

Democratic centralism is the political basis of Cuban society,[2] yet it is an inherently contradictory Leninist concept. On the one hand, its proponents advocate democracy, specifically participation in political life, which in Cuba means participation in the building of socialism, in mass organizations, and in the representative organs of government. On the other hand, there is total centralism; ultimate power concerning all societal activities rests on the Comité Central of the national Party. The contradiction between the tenets of centralism and democracy is mirrored in the two most important organizational structures in Cuban society: the Party on the one hand and the government and mass organizations on the other hand. The Party is totally exclusionary, while the mass organizations and the Poder Popular organize and represent everyone or everyone in a group or category. In all organizations, however, the centralist idea is upheld, since they are all organized hierarchically and all are subordinate to the Party (cf. Bengelsdorf 1994).

Centralism and Hierarchy

The Partido Comunista de Cuba is the only political party in Cuba, and it and its representatives have ultimate power over all matters of policy. The Party is *el alma de la revolución* (the soul of the revolution), as the party program poetically states. For those who live in Cuban society, it is clear that the Party indeed is the most important institution. It is presented as the representative of all Cuban people and as a guarantor of just and good public policy.

[2]The concept of democratic centralism has changed from referring to the organization of the party to encompassing the social relationships of a society (Waller 1981). I use the term in the way it is used in Cuba, namely, to describe the ideological and organizational basis of the society as a whole.

The men and women who have posts in the Party have not been elected by popular vote but are selected by other Party members. The Party is thus a closed organization in which only members can take part. In the Party, in the Poder Popular, and in the mass organizations, higher political levels, which coincide with larger geographical areas, have supremacy over lower levels. This is also true of posts in the organizations. For example, the municipal Party organization has to adhere to the decisions of the provincial and national Party organizations. The first secretary can make decisions for cadres at the same party level but must follow orders from persons at higher levels. Although in other circumstances hierarchy is equated with inequality and seen as negative, for example, class differences in other societies, the Party hierarchy is presented as both just and necessary. Indeed, this organizational structure is seen as a prerequisite for a well-functioning society. This resembles the Leninist idea of "trade-union consciousness" (Lenin 1974), although this concept refers to a situation under capitalism, which reflects the belief that the members of masses are aware of only their immediate interests and have no wider class consciousness. Therefore, the elite Party has to lead the masses and formulate their ideological goals, always in their best interest. Many militantes claim that there is no need for other parties in Cuba since the Communist Party runs the country well, governs with wisdom, and cares for the people. An individual citizen should never reject or question the system because of its failures but should feel strengthened by his or her efforts to improve it.

To ordinary Cubans, the Party represents both a diffuse idea of power, and a very concrete institution. Since so many aspects of life are interpreted in political terms, the Party is the symbol of the state, and government but also has great importance administratively, morally, and ideologically. That the Party has such a strict order of command results in efficiency and speed in the execution of many practical matters. For one, the Party has the means and the power to achieve its goals. For another, it is vital in introducing ideological messages and campaigns, and through it new ideas can be spread very quickly. Through the Party organization and the mass media, a message can reach most citizens extremely efficiently.

There are other problems associated with centralism, however. It often leads to extreme bureaucracy, since the chain of command is strict and fixed. Unpleasant decisions are pushed further and further up the hierarchy, and the best way to get results is often to go directly to the top. Realizing one's initiatives is also difficult since there is always a risk of having one's initiative or decision revoked by someone at a higher level. Thus, it is safer and easier for "ordinary people" to leave decision making to authorized leaders. The most common and often the most efficient way of solving problems is to present them to one of the cadres of the Party or of the Poder Popular who have access to resources. Visiting the building that houses the Poder Popular (literally, the People's Power) in Limones one always encounters people waiting in the lobby or outside in the building's shadow to see politicians or employees. Here people come to request help with all manner of practical matters, from obtaining food for their carrier pigeons, to having a new roof built on the village school. The hierarchical system also ensures that those higher up have more access to information, which lessens the possibility that those at lower levels will be able to make decisions. This sometimes counteracts the message of the leaders that all people are needed to build a revolutionary society.

During all my time in Palmera, the Poder Popular was totally subordinate to the Party, often even in matters of daily practical importance in the municipality. In 1990, the Party signaled that the formal autonomy of the Poder Popular in practical, political matters would be improved and it was announced at a meeting that delegates of the Poder Popular would have greater autonomy. That changes in the hierarchy of decision making are not always easy to implement is shown by the following story that a friend of mine told me: Queque, an illiterate but intelligent forestry worker from a village in the mountains and a delegate to the assembly of the Poder Popular, heard that the delegates were being encouraged to decide what should be done in their area so that all coffee could be harvested. Queque decided that four mules that normally were used in forestry in his village should be transferred for use during the coffee harvest. Alberto, the leader of the forestry work in the village, became furious and turned to the boss at the forestry department in Limones, who ordered that the mules be used in forestry. They also called the vice president of the Poder Popular, who agreed with the boss at the forestry department and said that the Poder Popular had not given any orders to transfer the mules. Alberto got a paper with the vice president's order, which he waved in front of Queque, who could not read it, and demanded to have his mules returned. Queque then walked the long way down to Limones and talked to the vice president. The vice president said that he could not revoke his decision, so Queque went to the first secretary of the Party. The first secretary told the vice president that he should not have undermined Queque's decisions. The vice president defended himself, saying that he had not recognized Queque as a delegate. The first secretary replied that the vice president in any case should have told Queque that they would solve the problem together since this was the new policy. It was decided that the various parties would have a meeting to do just that.

I do not know the result of that meeting, but probably the parties agreed to a compromise. The political hierarchy was so natural to the leaders that they did not even stop to consider that the situation had changed in any way. The final decision was made at the usual level—the highest one.

Leadership

It was no coincidence that the leader of the ceremony on the bridge was a man. In the municipality of Palmera, as in other parts of Cuba, only a handful of women hold top political positions.[3] A witty journalist once called the Cuban political system a system of "machismo-leninismo" (Fernandez 1991). Although this was meant to be a pointedly sarcastic comment, the revolution has been and still is very much a male enterprise. Many of the traits of the ideal revolutionary build on such traditional male traits as courage, virility, strength, audacity, and initiative (cf. Leiner 1994: 25). The idea of the man as protector, provider, and lover has also become a political

[3]There was only one woman in a top position in the Party during my fieldwork. In the ANAP, the two top positions belonged to men, and the same was true of the CDR, while in the CTC the leading position was held by a woman and the second position by a man. Naturally, the FMC had two women at the top. Most of the persons elected to political posts were also men.

ideal (cf. Gilmore 1990: 4). A good leader is a protector of society and a provider of the common good, which he is presumed to distribute as fairly as possible. He is the soldier who bravely goes to war for his country but also someone who helps others who are less fortunate, thereby showing manliness.

Leaders and militantes volunteer to do the toughest and the most risky jobs and take on the tasks the Party gives them without complaint. Using one's strength to create a just society is a revolutionary ideal transferred from the Party to the people.

A good revolutionary and a good leader is also what Cuban people describe as "a typical Cuban". Such a man also is an audacious, vivacious man with an insatiable appetite for laughing, making love, and enjoying himself—in short, for living.

The role of lover might seem to be a totally private one, but much of what this role stands for is also an important part of the public image for men. The Cuban lover is seen as autonomous, strong, sexually active, charming, and a conquerer, everything any man, including a political man, should be.

Cuba's female leaders are subject to the same ideals as its male leaders, but few Cubans expect women to live up to these ideals. On the contrary, women in higher political offices are sometimes viewed with suspicion, especially by men, for having "male" characteristics. They are seen as having reached their positions through sexual liasions. Although it might be true that some women use their sexuality to further their positions, men also do that, albeit in different ways. Also in political contexts men and women act in accordance with prescribed gender ideals. Thus, for women it is not so much a question of "sleeping around" as of flirting, acting complacent, and refraining from always voicing ones opinions, in other words of not "being difficult," as the men would see it. By contrast, men use sex to show they are "potent,"[4] and worthy of prestigious positions.

I have never heard anyone refer to political ideals in female terms. That a Cuban leader should be motherly or soft is unthinkable. Politicians are by definition potent; to be a good politician, one has to

[4]Lourdes Casal in her dissertation on Cuban novelists says that "to launch an accusation of homosexuality against a political enemy was one of the most terrible insults" (quoted in Leiner 1994:23). This is still true today.

have cojones (testicles, "balls"). Many men and some women also feel that women are not capable of being leaders, or at least that being a leader would make the woman less female. A woman is expected to be soft, caring, and based in the home. This can sometimes hold a woman back from trying to get ahead in public life. During my time in Palmera, only two women held top positions in the Poder Popular and the Party combined.

The heroes of the revolution are also seen as the embodiments of the male ideal. Living heroes from the revolutionary war are not monumentalized in Cuba. There are no statues or idols of Fidel Castro.[5] Two men, however, both of whom died early in the revolution, are honored in monuments and ceremonies: Che Guevara and Camilo Cienfuegos. Che Guevara, the Argentinian doctor who joined Fidel Castro in the struggles in the Sierra Maestra, is seen as the intellectual, the romantic, the good, an example of someone who sacrificed for the people, whereas Camilo Cienfuegos is the epitome of the Cuban man. He is often portrayed in a cowboy hat, with a big grin on his face. He is remembered as the witty, the brave, the almost reckless soldier, a manual worker with a gut instinct for military strategy. Together they symbolize the perfect man, who combines the best of physical and intellectual qualities.[6]

The revolutionary war was indeed very much a male affair, although women were involved in the urban struggle[7] and in the struggles in the Sierra Maestra. The leaders of the revolution, however, were and are almost exclusively men.

Only four women are considered major heroes, and although they are connected to the struggle through their own activities, they are known mainly as the wives, sisters, and companions of prominent

[5]Everywhere in the streets and in homes, though, there are photographs, clippings from magazines, and posters with photographs of such revolutionary heroes as Fidel, Che, and Camilo Cienfuegos.

[6]The two are celebrated together during a week in October highlighted by a beautiful ceremony in which children and adults throw flowers in the sea. This idea that man has two sides is presented through the two brothers in the excellent novel *The Mambo Kings* by Oscar Hijuelos (1989).

[7]Before Fidel Castro came back to Cuba and started the struggles in the Sierra Maestra in 1956, there were well-organized battles and sabotage in the cities; these continued up to the victory in 1959 and involved female revolutionaries.

male leaders. One of these women is Vilma Espín,[8] the wife of Raúl Castro. She made a place for herself in the revolution by becoming the general secretary of the FMC and a member of the central committee of the Party, among other important roles. Another woman, maybe the most beloved by the people, is Celia Sánchez, who in 1956 helped organize the reception for the boat *Granma*, which carried Fidel Castro and his men from Mexico to Cuba to start the revolution. Until her death in 1980, she was Fidel Castro's common-law wife, secretary, confidante, and adviser. Haydée Santamaría had a double and symbolically very strong connection to the revolution through two men—first through her brother Abel Santamaría, who was one of the leaders and martyrs of the urban struggle and killed by Fulgencio Batista's guardias in the Moncada attack in 1953, and, second through her husband, Armando Hart Dávalos, a fighter in the urban struggles and now minister of culture. Haydée Santamaría took part in the early revolutionary struggles and later was the director of the prestigious cultural organization Casa de las Américas until her suicide in 1980. The fourth female hero and fighter is Melba Hernández, already a friend of Fidel Castro before the Moncada attack, where she was arrested and imprisoned. Today she is a member of the Central Committee and head of the Center for Asian and Oceanian Studies. That these women are remembered mainly for their connections to male revolutionaries should not depreciate what they have done for the revolution, but their number shows that there were and are few channels for women to attain power and that very few women are seen as symbols of the revolution (cf. Bengelsdorf 1988: 126–29).

Jorge Domínguez (1978: 337) says in his book on Cuba that "the chief claims to legitimate rule in Cuba derive not from election but from the quality of the rulers and the way they rule." The best person should be the leader; this person should also behave exemplarily and has high and strict demands placed on him or her. This is true not only of rulers at higher levels but of leaders and indeed militantes in general. In many ways this notion is similar to the idea of the enlightened despot who rules for the best benefit of his people. Fidel Castro has always been "el líder maximo," the highest and undis-

[8]Here, of course, I use real names.

puted leader of the revolution, and in spite of the continuously stronger role of the Party, he has increasingly gained an almost mythical aura.[9] His omnipresence in Cuban society is emphasized in the many ways in which he is addressed: Fidel (never Castro); *El Comandante*, his title from the revolutionary war but also a symbolic way of conveying his ultimate position; *Comandante en Jefe* (commander in chief), which is his military rank but sometimes also used today as a way to emphasize his ultimate power; *nuestro jefe* (our boss), depicting both familiarity and subordination; and, sometimes, *nuestro papá* (our dad), even more connoting subordination, respect, and intimacy.[10]

A salient feature of the Cuban socialist ideology is that the leadership is expected to be active, which is also a male ideal. Leaders' positions in the political hierarchy are important, so that those highest up in the Party are also the most active, but all leaders are expected to lead actively. The leaders scold, criticize, and give directions as well as encouragement and praise. They often join in discussions, explaining and putting a more ideological cast on a question. One very common way of meeting criticism from people is for a leader to ask what they have done (cf. Moore 1977: 161). Leaders thereby urge people to take more responsibility, make more effort, and participate more in the process of "building the revolution," as it is phrased. Leaders also see their "leading" role as extending to matters that are not directly political. A female dirigente, for example, scolded the workers at the local hair dressers for not keeping the workplace tidy enough. They defended themselves but did not seem surprised by the incident.

[9]Even though the Party was formed in 1965, it did not take on a leading role immediately. The leadership of the country was then organized around Fidel and the leaders from the Sierra Maestra. Today the Party has a strong position, but Fidel Castro still holds the three most important posts in Cuba. He is commander in chief, president of the councils of state, and first secretary of the Communist Party of Cuba (see Brenner et al. 1989).

[10]There are also negative ways to refer to Fidel, for example by calling him *El Caballo* (the Horse), which I have never heard but have seen referred to; by making a gesture in which one passes the thumb and forefinger down around the chin, indicating a beard; or by referring to him as *El* (he/him).

Spreading the Party's ideological message is seen as a pedagogical task. Thus, the role of the Party and its cadres is to lead but also to teach the values and attitudes of socialism. The Party program (*Programa del PCC* 1987: 56–65) emphasizes the pedagogical and moral role of the Party. Words such as *formación, educación* (education, teaching), *confrontación* (confrontation), *lucha* (struggle), *crítica* (criticism), and *divulgación* (dissemination) express the principal aspects of this ideological work as the education of the workers to a higher political consciousness, the teaching of communist values to new generations, and the struggle against weak attitudes toward the socialist ideology. The Party program is, of course, the guiding star in the daily work of the leaders in Palmera, but mostly these leaders connect their pedagogical and ideological tasks with practical matters in the life of the municipality.

At a meeting of the local FMC in a small, remote village in Palmera, Rosa, the president of the municipal FMC, was present. The women in the local group were mostly agricultural workers and housewives who others would consider to have a fairly low cultural and educational level. They were strongly opinionated, however, taking examples from their own, often hard, lives. Rosa listened and sometimes offered an explanation or a commentary. At the end of the meeting, she asked the women about different political leaders. She handled the situation as a teacher might. She asked if they knew who the first secretary of the municipality was. The women looked at one another questioningly. "Nooo," they said, "he has not been here to visit." After a while, a woman remembered and said: "Well, come to think of it, there was a chap who came here to the beach in a jeep early one morning. It must have been around six o'clock. That must have been him. He asked my daughter if she knew who el Che was. And she knew, of course," she said proudly. Rosa said that it was probably the first secretary and asked if they knew his name. The women did not know. When Rosa stated his name, the secretary wrote it down, asking her to repeat his second surname because she had already forgotten it. After a while, Rosa asked once more what his name was and now the women remembered. She also asked the names of the president of the Poder Popular and others, but the women did not know their names either. The only leader they knew by name was the first secretary of the province. "He is a huge man," said one woman. The women did not seem to think it was very important to know these leaders' names, but Rosa said that they should know them. "These are our leaders," she said. Afterward she expressed concern to me that the women did not know the names of such important people.

Interrogation is a very common method leaders use to communicate with people and to check on what people know about something that is seen as important. Some people resent this style and feel intimidated. But many also feel that it is a good way for the leaders to keep people on their toes, especially when the interrogation is focused on someone else and even more when the subject is a low-level leader.

Sometimes leaders display a truly paternalistic attitude. The president of the Poder Popular in Palmera, a man in his late fifties, grew up in the area. He helped the rebels during the revolutionary war and had been a manual worker. He had been a politician for a long time and was both loved and disliked in the community—loved for his "simple" ways and his enormous ability to work, disliked for his habit of being very tough and demanding as much of others as of himself, but primarily for making decisions for people and not always hearing people out. Presiding at the municipal assembly, he often interrupted people and ordered them to be more concrete and brief when, as he said, he felt they were talking just for the sake of hearing their own voices. He also often rephrased motions for people who had spoken, and they seldom protested.

Sometimes politicians also make statements that go against the idea that everyone should be able to participate in the political process. During a meeting at which one of the highest politicians in the municipality was present, the recurring issue of the need for a day-care center in Palmera came up. A man spoke in favor of the center and wanted to make a proposal to build one. He used the women's argument which had been used over many years, that there were so many women who wanted to work and such difficulties with child care since not everyone had a relative who could look after a child. It would be good for the economy of the municipality to build a day-care center, he said. Before he could say more, the politician intervened and said there was no cause even to mention the day-care center because there was no money to build it now. The man who had raised the issue accepted this, and there was no discussion.

Party Members

According to the tenets of centralism, the leaders but also the militantes have an extremely large number of obligations, as well as responsibility and power, since they are the ones making the decisions and defining the "right ways" of thinking concerning many aspects of Cuban life.

About two thousand Palmerans are in the Party, or 14 percent of the adult population,[11] compared with the average of 10 percent for the country (Brenner et al. 1989: 173). To become a member of the Party or of the UJC, one has to be selected. A person may be suggested at his or her workplace or ask to become a member, and then the process leading to selection starts. If the person is considered a good worker, a loyal workmate, a good neighbor, and generally a decent person, he can become a member for a trial period of one year. If the *aspirantes*, as they are called, work out well and behave in the manner of militantes, they are given the membership book of the Party or of the UJC. The Cuban Communist Party, says its manual, organizes "the best children of the people, selected from the most distinguished obreros [workers], peasants, and other manual and intellectual workers who actively work for the materialization of the goals formulated in its program"[12] (*Estatutos del PCC* 1986:v).

Being a militante involves many duties but also has advantages. Militantes must be examples to others and remain totally loyal to the Party or the UJC. This means not only defending and spreading the ideas of the Party but also behaving in an exemplary manner in all aspects of life. Their conduct is discussed in meetings of the base group at their workplace. They are supposed to be critical and self-critical, both within the Party and in other areas of life. If they crit-

[11]This information is from militantes in Palmera. In addition, the UJC, the youth organization, has about one thousand members.

[12]All quotations from the *Estatutos del PCC* and the *Programa del PCC* have been translated by the author.

icize a person in an official capacity, they must always mention him by name and formulate the criticism so that the person being criticized can answer the allegations. This does not apply only to militantes; everyone is urged not to criticize behind the backs of others. Militantes are expected to accept any post the Party suggests for them, and their ultimate responsibility is always the Party. If they do not follow the rules of the Party, they can be given various sanctions, from a reprimand by their base group to exclusion from the Party. Among the advantages of being a militante are that one has greater access to information since there are often meetings at which Party cadres discuss news from the national or provincial level of the Party. Militantes are sworn to secrecy, so that information that may be dangerous or problematic is not revealed to the public until it is deemed appropriate. Party statutes say that the militante must "jealously guard the secrets of the Party and the state and keep proper discretion in other matters indicated to them" (*Estatutos del PCC* 1986: 7). Finally, militantes are expected to live model lives and, most important, must not cause public scandals.

Juana, a militante with an important political post, had trouble with her husband because he did not want to accept their divorce and kept coming back to their former house. If he drank, he arrived pounding on the door, shouting. When she opened, he was violent, pushing and shoving her. She was afraid of him and felt insecure in her house, but her biggest concern was that the scandal would affect her position as a militante and a political leader and cause her to lose her job and be expelled from the Party. She discussed this in her nucleo, and although the other militantes supported her and said they understood that the problem was not her fault, she continued to worry. That she was a woman probably increased Juana's worries, since there are so few women in politics in Palmera and behaving impeccably is therefore especially important. She also knew that women are more likely to be criticized than men when they are involved in a public scandal.

Militantes and leaders do not always lead impeccable lives, of course. The sanctions and reactions to their "flaws" are judged not only on the basis of the Party program or socialist ideology but on the basis of common cultural "folk models" of what it means to be a decent person. Being a womanizer does not fall into the category of bad behavior for a male leader as long as the behavior is within certain limits. When the limit has been surpassed, however, the sanctions are both personal and political.

Manuel, a young militante in the UJC and a cadre in one of the mass organizations, had a common-law marriage with Carmen, who was also a militante. Like most men in Palmera, Manuel was seeing other women en la calle. One night he overstepped the boundaries of respectability. He had been seeing a young girl for some time, and they had met at an outdoor party in Limones. After having danced for a while, they went to Manuel's workplace to be alone. Manuel's brother-in-law accompanied them to keep watch outside the office. While Manuel and his young lover were in the office making love, the brother-in-law, who thought that Manuel was going too far this time, went home to his sister, Carmen, and told her what was happening at the office. She was furious and knew that this was her chance to catch her erring husband in flagrante delicto. She and her brother went back to the office together, broke down the door, and found the two lovers in bed "como vinieron al mundo" (as they entered the world), as one of my informants said. There was a great commotion and the girl was sent to the bathroom to dress, where she took the opportunity to escape. Manuel's brother-in-law beat him up and told Manuel to get out of Palmera or he would be killed by Carmen's family. Afterward, Carmen filed a complaint with the youth organization about Manuel's behavior and requested that he be sanctioned. The UJC had already decided to sanction him. He was discharged from the UJC for one year, and his workplace sentenced him to work in the mountains. The UJC also sanctioned Carmen, however, because she had exposed the scandal and helped break down the door to the office.

This incident would not have been more than an item of general gossip had Manuel not used the office as a meeting place. He combined two otherwise compatible principles, the importance of being a respectable and trustworthy militante and cadre—an example to others—and of being a real man, sexually active and full of lust. In this case, however, Manuel was indiscreet, but more importantly he was disrespectful of a political arena by exposing it to public scandal. Ultimately, the political principle had to take precedence over the personal.

Socialist Democracy

The Party program of the PCC talks about the need for Cuba to become a "socialist democracy," which is said to be "incomparably superior to bourgeois democracy" (*Programa del PCC* 1987: 65). Cuban socialist democracy involves participation and equality, and the Party program expresses the goal of this democracy as "the increase in participation of all people in state management and in popular control, in the political and social life of the country, and in the unfolding of the creative initiatives of the masses in all spheres of society, particularly in the production of material goods and the development of new cultural values" (ibid.: 65). Thus, the main feature of Cuban democracy is the active participation of all citizens in social matters. As we have seen, opportunities to take creative initiative are often counteracted by the centralist political structure, although there are ways for the citizenry to take part individually in political decisions. Here participation in elections and the bi-yearly meeting with the delegate will be discussed; other acts of participation are covered in chapter 6.

The avenue whereby the most Cubans can influence politics is the elections to the Poder Popular. In Palmera, the Poder Popular was introduced in 1976. The municipality is divided into different constituencies, and each elects a delegate to the asamblea municipal. This assembly meets approximately every second month, and its purview is matters of importance to the whole municipality.[13]

Before the election, every constituency has a meeting to nominate candidates to represent the constituency. Both militantes and non-Party members may be nominated, and anyone may suggest a candidate. There are some restrictions, however, since all candidates must be screened by the Party, which means that no known critics of the system are ever accepted. Since there is only one party, candidates are nominated based on their personal qualifications. Quite a few non-Party members are elected, who represent differing views

[13]The executive committee of the Poder Popular is composed of the president, the vice president, and three other cadres—a secretary, an economist, and a person responsible for sports, education, and culture. The president is appointed by the asamblea. The other posts are divided between the committee members themselves.

within the Party framework. Before the election, photographs and a biography of each candidate are displayed, usually on a bulletin board in the constituency. In Palmera this step is a bit superfluous, because most people in the constituency know each other. There were two candidates in "my" constituency in 1989: the former delegate, a woman, who is also a professional in the Poder Popular, and a male cadre in one of the mass organizations. Both were militantes.

Days before the election in 1989, newspapers, television, and radio, the Party, and cadres urged people to vote early in the morning so that the results would be ready by nightfall. On the morning of the election, cars with loud speakers arrived at 5:00, blaring out loudly that everyone should vote early. The polling stations opened at 6:30, and by 7:00, when I went to the station, some of my neighbors had already been to vote. At the polling station, officials were busy checking identity cards and ticking off the voters on a list. At the ballot box, two pioneros stood guard by the Cuban coat of arms and the flag. When each voter had cast his or her vote, the pioneros saluted and said, "¡Votó!" People were coming to the station in a constant stream, but after some time there was only a trickle and then no one. A couple of the pioneros were sent out to knock on the doors of those who had not yet voted and urge them to come to vote. By 3:30 in the afternoon, everyone had voted, and the votes were counted. Juana, the incumbent delegate, received sixty-four votes; Luis received forty-seven. Voting figures were high for the municipality and 98 percent in the country (*Granma*, 2 Jan. 1989). In Palmera, eighty-one candidates were elected.

Elections are voluntary and secret, and in smaller towns and villages people know the candidates personally. The social control is strict in urging people to vote, and the only way of showing discontent is to cast a blank vote, to avoid voting by leaving town, or to stand up for the right not to vote.

Meeting with the Delegate

Another way of participating in decision making, probably the most important way of all, is by attending the biyearly *rendición de cuenta* (meeting with the delegate) in each constituency (cf. Bengelsdorf 1994).

The person elected to deal with the problems of a neighborhood is its delegate to the municipal assembly of the Poder Popular. This delegate is well known, and the members of a constituency often take the opportunity to talk to him or her in the street or on private occasions. Each delegate also has *despacho*, hours when he meets with constituents at his home. In my constituency, the delegate was available every Tuesday night. Few people visited during these hours, and at the public meeting the delegate complained that issues would have been addressed more easily and quickly if people had come with their complaints during the weekly despacho.

At the biyearly rendición de cuenta, all members of the constituency are invited to bring forward complaints and suggestions about their neighborhoods. The delegate also renders an account of what he or she has done about matters discussed at the previous meeting. These meetings are lively, and ideas and complaints are discussed with gusto and good humor. There is always much laughter. Some matters are mentioned at every meeting, but several are dealt with and reported on, and new matters are are addressed as well.

The *planteamientos* (formal complaints), very often concern the lack of consumer goods in the country. In a mountain village, one of the most important issues was the lack of batteries for transistor radios. The radio is a vital part of everyday life here, since villagers do not have electricity and therefore no TVs. "If the radio does not work, we do not get any news, and we cannot hear music either. Then it's really bad," said one man. People reported that the shop had batteries but not the right kind for the radios.

In Limones, concerns about meat distribution were voiced time and time again. In 1988, Raúl, a chauffeur, wanted an additional meat shop in his area. The existing one was too small, and the police had to come every time meat was distributed (every second week) and form two lines, one for men, one for women; otherwise they fight, he said. Raúl thought that one more shop would improve the situation. Catalina, a cadre in one of the mass organizations, added that there were times when there was not enough meat for everyone. Since there was only half a pound for each person every second week, it was a catastrophe when one missed out, she said. "That makes it a month between meat times." This happened mostly to the women who worked, because it was more difficult for them to get to the shop during the three days when meat was available. Catalina proposed that meat be distributed for more days and that the distribution system be improved. Everyone agreed that there had to be better organization. At another meeting, someone said that the meat was often bad, that it had even been green, and that it frequently was not fit for eating. The delegate wrote down the complaints and said that she would see what could be done.

When I returned two years later, in 1990, the quality of the meat in Limones had improved, but it was still bad at times and there were still lines at the meat shop. Complaints continued about the pescadería, the shop where fish, eggs, and meat were sold. Carmen wanted the shop to be open on Sundays, when the meat was distributed. Many women work, she said, and do not have time to go to the pescadería on Friday and Saturday, and on Monday the meat is frozen and cannot be bought until the afternoon. People giggled about the eternal problem of the pescadería. The delegate said that there had been discussion about keeping the shop open till 8:00 or 9:00 at night when the meat was distributed. Someone also suggested that the shop sell fish, eggs (when there were any), and other items when meat was sold. At the time one could not buy these commodities when meat was sold. The delegate said that she would check on that.

Although the system of meat distribution still did not function adequately in 1990, other complaints had been resolved. At one meeting, the delegate said that of twenty-one complaints, fourteen had been resolved. The delegate reminded her constituents that "we Cubans are very good at complaining and gossiping about others, but we do not think about how we ourselves act." She also reminded the constituents that the coffee harvest was in full progress and that few constituents had agreed to voluntary work. "And you know that we need all the foreign currency we can get for the coffee," she said. "We use all the things that the revolution has given us—schools, hospitals, buses, roads—but we do not think that to receive one also has to give. If we want to have things in the shop, we must pick coffee." The delegate also complained about the poor participation in the activities related to the Día de la Defensa. A woman who was considered a little simple by the others was extraordinarily outspoken and said that she was sure that people knew about the activities but that they did not *want to* participate. People giggled and, embarrassed, looked down at the floor.

A delegate who wants to stay in office must convince the people of his or her abilities by resolving complaints. The atmosphere at meetings is often very open, and the relationship between the delegates and the constituents is one of equality. Delegates "educate" the people in the way that politicians do, by urging them to sacrifice for the revolution, but that does not seem to destroy the tenor of equality. How the meeting is conducted depends a lot on the delegate but also on the constituents. I had the feeling that the rendición de cuenta in the constituency where many of the dirigentes (leaders) and cadres lived was more of a formality, because they had so many other ways of solving local problems.[14] In other constituencies, where there were mostly workers and farmers, the biyearly meeting was more important and people saw it as the principal way of getting things accomplished.

Most people are very dependent on their delegate, and when the delegate functions badly, there are consequences. In Las Minas, a village on the coast of Palmera, people were very dissatisfied with their delegate. He had not done what he should, they said, and he was never available when they needed him. He was not present at one rendición de cuenta, allegedly because of illness in his family, and another delegate from nearby chaired the meeting. No one explicitly expressed any criticism of the delegate at the meeting, but from what people said in discussing a variety of issues, it was clear that they were very displeased with him. When the chairman read the report from the delegate about the meeting half a year before and listed which issues had been resolved, a man raised his hand and said that there were two issues that were not mentioned in the report and that remained outstanding. "We have complained about this many, many times," he said, "and nothing has happened." The two issues—the lack of electricity and the need to repair the water pipes—in the village were added to the report. When the chairman asked if the constituents could accept the report, the man who had just spoken said that he could only "partially" accept it, because he

[14]Since many of the dirigentes came from other parts of the province or country, they lived in the first multifamily housing constructed in Limones.

felt it was a grave error that the issues had not been included in the original document. Others murmured consent. This was very severe criticism, and it was evident that the delegate would have difficulty getting reelected.

People are very outspoken in these meetings, and many voice complaints. The women are as vocal as the men, and sometimes more so. Militantes and leaders in the community are more likely to voice complaints, and sometimes the militantes meet before the rendición to agree on which ones to present or which not to present. For example, they might agree not to present an issue that the Party wants to suspend for the time being for ideological or practical reasons. Since the formal complaints are not previewed, however, other participants at the meetings can bring up an issue that the militantes agreed to avoid.

Equality

Equality is an important feature of socialist democracy, although the term *igualdad* is seldom used singularly but is qualified in various ways. Equality is emphasized in the relationship between the leaders and the people. It was an ideal set by Fidel Castro and others at the beginning of the revolution (cf. Lockwood 1990) and is advocated by today's leaders. Leaders dress simply; Fidel is always in an olive-green uniform. In Palmera, the leaders wear mostly jeans or other casual trousers and a shirt, or a guayabera if the situation is more formal. The term of address introduced after the revolution—*compañero, compañera*—is used to address everyone. In that the concept of *respeto* (respect or courtesy) is very important, most people in Palmera address leaders with the formal *usted* in official situations or if they do not know them personally, but the manner of speaking and the interaction are informal and relaxed.

Terms of address can vary contextually. One evening, while visiting a friend in Palmera, I heard her talking to someone on the phone, joking and laughing and using the familiar *tú* and a nickname. I was surprised to learn that the person she was talking to was the first secretary in Palmera, whom she always addressed as *usted* and *compañero* when we met him under official circumstances. Her explanation was that they knew each other very well, were friends, and had worked together for a long time but that in more official situations she wanted to show respect for his position.

The Party program quotes a speech by Fidel Castro in which he talks about the virtues for Party members and leaders of *sencillez* (sincerity and modesty). The quotation includes the slogan of the Party: "Never above the masses, always with the masses and always in the heart of the people!" (*Programa del PCC* 1987: 71). The leader ideally does not have any advantages from his post but has a heavy workload and a lot of responsibility. In Palmera there is very little difference between the leaders and other people. The leaders who come from the area know most of the inhabitants of Palmera and have very personal relationships with many as friends, neighbors, schoolmates, and relatives. The first secretary in Palmera, for example, lives in a two-room apartment with his wife and child and two relatives. He and other higher dirigentes have access to a car with a chauffeur, and often they have telephones, which are uncommon in Palmera. Their greatest privilege is that they can obtain goods and information much easier than others because of their position and therefore are attractive partners in reciprocal relationships.

Equality is an important concept in Cuban socialism, but it does not connote similarity, as it does, for example, in Sweden (Ekman 1991; Rosendahl 1985). Rather, it means equal opportunities for all.[15] This has been realized in the areas of medicine and education, in the right and duty for everyone to work and in the rationing system. In these areas, all Cubans have the same rights. The first secretary in Palmera, however, emphasized in a speech that differences do and should exist.[16]

> We have to aspire to do more, but we will never be able to make a society that is totally equal. That is a lie; that will never happen. We try to create a society that is the most just society possible. But it is not perfect and not egalitarian. That is what we try to do, but many people do not understand that. People think that everyone can be the same. No, señor, the doctor can never be the same and never get the same as, for example, a cowhand, even if he is the best possible and improves the situation for others. The doctor has another nivel, another

[15]Pat Caplan (1993) observed a similar view of equality in Tanzania.

[16]Other parts of this speech will be closly examined in the next chapter.

> status, recognized in society. So although the two have the same opportunity, there will always be a difference. The doctor, the engineer, the professional are different, and it should be like that. No one is the same, not even in nature. Look, I have five fingers on my hand, and none of those five fingers are the same, but all are fingers. So if we aspire to and idealize an egalitarian society, we will frankly lead to the destruction of this society, because equality will not exist. A more just society, yes, so that everyone has the right to education, to work, to retirement, to an eight-hour workday, to go to whichever shop, beach, restaurant they want, anywhere they want, and society guarantees equal justice for everyone. But there will always be something in the system that is not equal, that is *not* equal. There are many compañeros who get mixed up, but it cannot be like that [total equality].

By using the metaphor of his hand, the first secretary explained the impossibility, indeed the undesirability, of having a totally egalitarian society. He emphasized that he wanted a just society with equal opportunities for all but not a society where everyone, for example, has equal salaries. Those who give a lot to society also should be rewarded. This builds on the supposition, expressed on other occasions, that Cuban society has still not become communist, the goal of Marxist-Leninist ideology. It is now in the phase of socialism, and although the society has changed a lot for the better, differences still exist between manual workers and intellectuals, city and countryside. As expressed in the program of the Party (*Programa del PCC* 1987: 25), work is still a means of survival and workers need material as well as moral incentives to perform. An interesting nuance here is that the first secretary also seemed to regard differences in status as necessary. He talked about the "nivel" of the better educated. This is a word that implies both formal education and what the Cubans call cultura, being refined and cultivated. The implication was that he thought there would always be status differences in Cuban society. Although I have never heard it expressed so directly before, this view is compatible with the view that equality could not exist without the hierarchy of the Party. Within the framework of the revolution, it is the Party that has made equality possible.

View of Palmera

On 26 July and New Year's Eve the red and black banner of the 26 July Movement and the white, blue, and red national flag are displayed on façades and from balconies in Palmera. Here, to celebrate 26 July 1995, the flags together with portraits of Fidel Castro, Che Guevara, and Camilo Cienfuegos are placed on the porch of a private house in Limones.

In the Sierra Maestra mountains mules are the best means of transportation. A string of mules transports coffee from the farm where it has been picked to a warehouse where the coffee-berries will be dried.

On a Sunday in October 1989 voluntary workers collected rocks from the beach. The rocks were used to build a junior high school in a village in the western part of Palmera.

Rita cooks in her small and rather dark kitchen in Limones. She has prepared rice and beans, plantains, and some beef on the kerosene stove, which she lights with alcohol.

[5]

Talking about the Revolution

After concluding his speech, the second secretary of the Party stood silently for a few seconds, his head bent. He then looked up, scanned the crowd, and shouted at the top of his voice, "¡Patria o muerte!" (Homeland or death!). The crowd answered, "¡Venceremos!" (We shall win!). Voices were heard shouting "¡Viva Fidel, Viva el Partido!" and the crowd answered "¡Viva!." Fists were raised in the air. The second secretary then added in a stentorian voice: "¡Socialismo!" and the audience answered: "¡O muerte!" (Or death!).

These slogans are used in all speeches, although they represent shifts in emphasis during the recent history of Cuba.[1] From the turn of the century, Cuba had been totally dependent on the United States, both economically and politically. Corruption and political violence were widespread, and the American mafia controlled drugs, prostitution, and gambling in Havana. Class differences were significant, and many of the campesinos in the countryside lived miserable lives. In the 1950s, protests grew against the oppressive Batista regime, and students and young workers committed acts of sabotage and demonstrated in the cities. On 26 July 1953, Fidel Castro led the attack on the Moncada garrison in Santiago de Cuba. The attack was a military failure and many of the attackers were killed, but the event is treated as the ideological beginning of the revolution.

[1]For reviews of the historical development of Cuba after 1959, see, for example, Bengelsdorf 1994; Brenner et al. 1988; Kapcia 1992; Pérez 1988; Pérez-Stable 1994.

While still in prison after the Moncada attack, Fidel wrote his defense speech, which became the program for the revolution. He turned to the masses "to whom everyone makes promises but who everyone cheats and deceives" (Castro 1983:31), promising to solve the problems with the land, industrialization, housing, unemployment, education, and health (ibid.:36). The emphasis was on the need to defend la patria and advance national independence, democracy, and social justice (Brenner et al. 1989:35–41).

The revolutionary leaders, of whom Fidel Castro was the most outstanding, were inspired by José Martí and his humanistic views. They wanted to throw off the yokes of colonialism and imperialism, which after Spanish rule had meant almost total dependence on the United States (Brenner et al. 1989; Pérez 1988). People had increasingly resented the cruelty shown by President Batista and his soldiers and were happy to support a new, and, they hoped, fair political alternative (Brenner et al. 1989:145). The Movimiento 26 de Julio, an ideologically diverse organization named for the date of the Moncada attack, led the uprising with fierce struggles in the cities.

In 1956, Fidel Castro and his men ended their exile in Mexico and landed in the yacht *Granma* on the southeast coast of Cuba. The struggle which began in the Sierra Maestra mountains, would lead to the triumph of the revolution. The local people considered the rebels, as they were called, fair and trustworthy, and the army grew from a handful of men to quite a few in a short time. As the fighting continued, other leaders besides Fidel Castro were made comandantes. Among them were Che Guevara, Camilo Cienfuegos, Juan Almeida (the only black comandante), and Fidel's younger brother, Raúl. By 1958, the rebels had won so much territory that they were marching toward Havana forcing the dictator, Fulgencio Batista, to flee the country together with many others from the bourgeoisie.

On 1 January 1959, Fidel announced the victory of the revolution in Santiago de Cuba, and on 5 January he gave his well-known speech in Havana, declaring the aims of the new leadership. While Fidel was speaking, white doves were released, symbolizing the new era, and two came to sit on his shoulders. The roars and cheers from the crowd seemed as if they would never cease.[2] Today many Cubans recall this as a highly symbolic, almost mythic event.

At the beginning of the 1960s, after the "constructive friendship" (Brenner et al. 1989:41) with the United States government had failed, a closer relationship developed with the Soviet Union and Cuba shifted to a socialist policy. Although adhering rhetorically to a Marxist-Leninist ideology, a democratic centralist organization and a one-party system, Cuba suffered from both political and economic disorganization and was extremely dependent on Castro and his charismatic leadership. Many professionals and businessmen left the country when socialism was declared. The most politically astute Cubans were the former communists (ibid.:157), who soon took over many leading positions, which led to political conflicts. A repressive political period followed, worsened by many counterrevolutionary activities both from outside and within the country, of which the Playa Girón (Bay of Pigs) invasion was only the most well known abroad. Up to this point la patria was definitely the most important ideological symbol. To defend the homeland or die was not only a slogan but a reality for many people.

After many difficulties and political mistakes, as well as an increase in the national standard of living, the Party slowly consolidated its place in Cuban society. In 1975 (ibid.:167), the first Party congress was held. And although lately some of the tasks of the Party have been delegated to other institutions, such as the Poder Popular, in practice, the Party is still the most important institution in Cuba.

The use of the more dramatic slogan "¡Socialismo o muerte!" was introduced in the late 1980s and was soon used throughout the country as a symbolic defense of the existing policy. In view of the wavering of socialist ideals in Eastern Europe and the introduction of glasnost and perestroika in the Soviet Union, Fidel announced that Cuba would never abandon socialism. The slogan was also used to support adaptation to the country's worsening material conditions. In his 26 July 1988 speech in Santiago de Cuba, Fidel defended at length Cuba's road to socialism but emphasized that Cuba must build it in its own way. "Now we will continue to seek nuestro camino [our

[2] At the Museum of the Revolution in Havana, a film is shown of this event, and it is also sometimes shown on television.

own way] . . . and we will always stubbornly refuse to slavishly copy the remedies for illnesses which we have not suffered" (Castro 1988: 53). He also said that "socialism is not created spontaneously; socialism has to be constructed, and the essential tool in the construction of socialism is the Party (ibid.:59).[3]

Language of the Revolution

In Palmera, a salient feature of everyday life is that both political leaders and ordinary people constantly refer to the revolution and to the ideals of a socialist society. Socialism in Palmera is not identified primarily with Marxism-Leninism but with the social changes brought about as a result of the Cuban revolution. Marxist terms are very seldom used in official speeches, and ordinary people never use them. Militantes are taught Marxist theory in courses and children are taught the Marxist approach to history and society in school, but this is more as general background than as analytical concepts.

I attended an ideological meeting for the cadres of Cultura, (the municipal branch of the Ministry of Culture), where a professor of Marxism was speaking about "how to teach culture."[4] His speech recalled precisely many other speeches I had heard during my fieldwork. The professor talked about culture and patriotism and the role of culture in the struggle against antisocial behavior and emphasized that the expressions of culture must teach respect for the society and socialist ideas. He concluded by telling the cadres that they must spread knowledge about dialectical materialism and study Marxism-Leninism. He did not explain how and when this process of education was going to take place. After the talk, no one asked any questions and people quickly left for their jobs. One of the cadres, who had a university degree, later expressed strong criticism of this speech and also of teaching at the university and stated that it was a mechanical

[3]At the fourth Party congress in 1991, it was agreed that the Party would share more of its responsibilities with the Poder Popular (Reed 1992). Even before that, in the fall of 1990, the number of cadres leading the Party in Palmera had been cut back.

[4]Here culture refers to theater, dance, painting, music, and so on.

Marxism that was taught that presented no possibilities to analyze it critically. I had the same experience in a night course in Cuban history at the high school level, in which, for example, the role of the Communist Party in Cuba in the early twentieth century appeared to be exaggerated.

Rather than Marxist-Leninist language, slogans and concepts that have been coined in the last thirty years are used frequently. The idea of the revolution is referred to by everyone, in all kinds of situations, and is defined in many different ways. The concept is so much a part of common knowledge that those who refer to it do not have to, and indeed often could not, define it in any simple way.

The term "revolution" is often equated with "society." When Cubans, leaders and masses alike, talk about the country's history after 1959, their society in general, and specific achievements and developments during this period, they often talk about what has happened "during the revolution." The "revolution" can also refer to the actual historical moment of the revolutionary war. The word *triunfar* (triumph) is used by almost everyone to refer to the victory of the revolution in 1959.

Implicit in the ideas presented by the leaders to the people is the idea that the revolution is ongoing. The revolution/society is not completed yet, the leaders say; it is going through a dialectical development, which explains the faults and mistakes that have occurred (see Rosendahl 1992a). Thirty years of revolution have not made Cuban society perfect. Implicit in this idea, of course, is the Marxist idea that societies evolve from socialist to communist. Although the emphasis here is on process, the revolution itself is often reified and talked about as a thing or a specific phenomenon. Leaders do not say that people have to sacrifice everything for their society but for the revolution. Proud citizens do not say "look what we have achieved" but "look what the revolution has given us." "Thanks to the revolution" is an expression many people use when talking about the good things they have experienced during the last thirty years (cf. Lancaster 1988). This can refer to the improved medical care, which all Cubans appreciate, or the access to education, or to other improvements in the standard of living. There is also a contradiction in this statement because ideally the revolution *is* the people. Without the people there would be no revolution. At the same time, the revolution is spoken of as a phenomenon apart from the people, as giving things to them and making things for them. This view is connected to the contradiction between democracy and centralism; thus, everyone is supposed to be creative and to use his or her initiative to build the society while at the same time obeying the Party.

For a long time in Cuba, the term "revolution" has been synonymous with "socialism" which in turn is closely related to the Party. In general discourse, the Party symbolizes the state, the Party organization, and the government. There is no talk about the "withering away of the state," as in classic Marxist-Leninist discourse on the state in a socialist society (Lenin 1964). The Party program establishes that the state is an expression of the interests of the working class in alliance with the peasants, a situation that makes Cuba "the most democratic state that has ever existed in the history of humanity" (*Programa del PCC* 1987:25).

At times revolutionary concepts are used to give legitimacy to conflicts. A conflict arose between a dirigente and some of the people who worked for him. He thought that they were lazy and not carrying out their jobs to his satisfaction. They felt that he was too inflexible and too authoritarian in his relationship to them and that they therefore could not do their jobs properly. The situation deteriorated over several months, and eventually blows were exchanged between the boss and one of his cadres. Subsequently, a rumor developed that two of the cadres had spoken in derogatory and sarcastic ways about Fidel and the Party. The boss then denounced these cadres and a few others to the Party and accused them of engaging in counterrevolutionary activities, a very serious accusation. This attack elevated the conflict from a personal quarrel to a political issue. The conflict was brought to court and the cadres were dismissed from their jobs because they had not fulfilled their work tasks, not for counterrevolutionary activities. There were political differences between the dirigente and the cadres. The cadres were young university students, some of them militantes in the UJC. They were outspoken and critical of much in society, while the dirigente was a middle-aged man, used to having a leading position; he was an intellectual but not a militante himself. This might have made him even more sensitive to being "politically correct." By turning the problem into an ideological issue, he emphasized his political awareness in the eyes of the Party and thereby shifted the emphasis away from the disciplinary problems. Verbal criticism of socialism is not a felony, however, so the court gave the cadres a very common sentence under such circumstances, namely the loss of their jobs.[5]

Rhetoric of the Leaders

The Party's ideological messages are spread locally through speeches, ceremonies, and face-to-face interactions. The ideas originating at the top of the Party, however, are always somewhat reformulated and changed by the time they reach the lower levels of the Party organization. As we shall see, local leaders tend to draw on the mutual experiences of their audience members when they talk about important matters.

In the fall of 1990, the Cuban economy suffered a hard blow, and the situation that the Cubans call el período especial began. Trade with Eastern Europe and the Soviet Union had long been the backbone of the Cuban economy. This was now made very difficult because of the emerging economic and political situation in these countries. The crises in Iraq affected oil and gasoline trade from that area. In Cuba, the free food market was closed and the gas ration was cut in half. A plan called El Programa Alimentario (the Food Program) was introduced by the government with the aim of producing more food locally. Fidel went around the country exhorting and inspiring people to grow vegetables and root crops and to raise animals wherever they could.

On the Day of the Agricultural Workers, their trade union in Limones organized a big party and ceremony for agricultural workers (mostly men), held at outdoor ceremonial grounds. Sixty or seventy workers came in flat-top trucks from all over the municipality and

[5]People who have not done anything criminal but who create problems for the political system by protesting or voicing inappropriate points of view are often excluded from participation in society by losing their jobs or other benefits. In this case, the cadres got new jobs after a while.

were given food and beer. As the men munched on pork casserole, yucca, and rice, and drank the beer, the festivities became loud, since many of the men knew each other but had not met in a long time and were now catching up on news from different parts of Palmera. The day was a scorcher, and everyone was sweating profusely. After a while, the organizers of the ceremony called the group to order, and the first secretary of the Party, the president of the Poder Popular, the head of the EMA, the state agricultural company, in Palmera, and the head of the agricultural union took their places under the shadow of a tree in front of the assembled crowd.

After medals had been distributed to the men who had worked for more than twenty-five consecutive years in agriculture and some speeches had been made, the people urged the first secretary to speak. The first secretary, Pedro, said that he had not planned on saying anything but then talked for half an hour. His speech illustrates well the political rhetoric one hears in Palmera and some of the topics that constantly are touched upon in speeches.

The first secretary talked about the difficult economic situation. Mixing references to practical matters with ideological and moral exhortations, he talked freely, without any script. He often repeated important words and phrases, a very common form of emphasis in Cuban speech.

> We are optimists. We see that the ideas of Fidel and of the Party have caught on. A few months back we were having some difficulties, because people did not understand [the situation], but now people seem to understand. People understand why we have to sow, why we have to cultivate. With the present economic situation, we have to rely on agriculture. We have to organize the workforce better; we have to really start using our coffee plantations. We have to prepare intelligently, with the resources we have, so that when the coffee harvest is over and the students are demobilized,[6] we can fill all those hostels [in the mountains] with mobilized people whom we will look for here in the municipality, among the people who are not working. If we have to ask for help from other municipalities, we will do that, but first of all we will use those here who do not work.

[6]Adults and schoolchildren are often sent to the countryside to work in agriculture. When the Programa Alimentario started, the mobilizations accelerated.

After presenting the problem, Pedro introduced a moral element into the speech—the ideas of honor and *cumplir* (fulfill obligations), a concept that is charged with moral connotations. He continued: "I think that anyone who does not work in these circumstances—that is immoral. We must see to it that all Cubans who feel useful and able should work and help their patria."

Pedro then talked about some young men who were doing their military service in the Ejército Juvenil del Trabajo.[7] They had promised to work in brigades in the Programa Alimentario, but few had shown up when they were called.

> It is not the right attitude in these times that a group of compañeros who promised, who gave their word, did not turn up *cumpliendo* [fulfilling their obligations]. We have to get used to keeping the word we give. I think that it is a thing of honor. If we say, for example, that we will sow ten *caballerías*[8] in La Granja today, we must not give up until we have achieved that. We must not expect things to be easy, as we have done before. Now we have to use everything we have; we have to take out the oxen, take out the carts; we have to use the intelligence of all of us workers, of all, of all the leaders. We [the leaders] have to explain to the workers. What we have to do this year is to put agriculture in the best of conditions. If we build all the hostels that we are planning and put people there, we can clean up all the coffee plantations so that no one can criticize us for the situation of the lianas, which is a problem every time people are going to pick coffee. We could have people there all the time, cleaning, pruning, doing everything. And that will give us more coffee, and more coffee means more foreign currency. The efforts we are making in the Programa Alimentario must not be lost. On the contrary, we have to increase them. There are good attitudes among people; there are compañeros who leave their easy work in other sectors and ask to be sent to agriculture, to lead brigades, to make up collectives.

Here Pedro talks about the difficult economic situation as, on the one hand, an organizational problem. The Party will solve the problem through organizing agricultural work in a better way. On the

[7]This is a part of the military organization in which young men perform their military service by working in agriculture.

[8]One caballería is approximately thirty-three acres.

other hand, the obstacle to this achievement, as he sees it, is primarily a moral one, the fact that some people do not *cumplir*. This he referred to as an immoral act, an act against the state and the revolution.[9] Pedro went on talking at length about the arrangements that would make it possible for people to work in the food program. He also talked about improving the conditions for the agricultural workers, for those working in the cow sheds, for example, where conditions were very bad. But then he came back to the moral aspect of the situation:

> You heard the words of Fidel in which he suggested that there are many things that will be changed in agriculture, like the salaries and other things. But all of that will have to get a response. If we pay more salaries and the workers keep on working only four hours a day, as many are doing now, we will not solve the problems. With higher wages we have to have more conscience, more devotion, and more demands from every one of the cadres leading agriculture and more contact between the leaders and the people. The leaders should constantly be checking, controlling, attending to the problems of the workers, always trying to find solutions to problems, inventing, because one has to invent. The capacity is not lacking, but at times it seems that *voluntad* [will] is lacking and sometimes the will is not encouraged [by the leaders].

Pedro went on to give an example from a workplace he had visited, something leaders often do to remind audiences of their knowledge of the area and their common experiences. Then one of the men listening, an agricultural worker from a mountain village, raised his hand and wanted to add something. Enrique used the respectful pronoun *usted*, when addressing the first secretary.

> ENRIQUE: If you permit me . . .
> PEDRO: Yes?!
> ENRIQUE: . . . I would like to say some words. We are good workers, and good farmers, but one little thing is necessary, that the brigade chiefs, the technicians that you send, that they make demands, because

[9]In 1990, a law against vagrancy was reactivated in Cuba. This law makes it possible for the state to prosecute those who refuse to take work that is offered them.

otherwise we are working completely alone. We are working because of our own conscience, but we do not have demands from someone who is there, you know, like before, *el capataz* [the foreman]. If I came an hour late before, well, *compay* [mate], I had to pay for those minutes. Because one has to work. Well, now we come and there are no bosses, I do what I want and I sit when I want, because there is no one who demands anything from me. Someone has to tell the technicians to be there, because that is necessary. And if they don't, send them back here. So that they can get a good whipping, because I am tired of this. [Laughs]. When I am working I'm trying to tell the compañeros [to work], but at times they just sit in the hostels. And if there is no one to tell them, they sit because they do not feel like struggling. They go to their hostel and don't do anything.

The relaxed atmosphere at the festival grounds, the physical closeness of the men standing around the first secretary, and maybe also the effects of the beer and the food made it easier for Enrique to speak up. Speaking up is not very common in other more formal situations, although people frequently give support to their leaders and at the same time offer a personal critique of a problem. The positive role of the prerevolutionary capataz might not have been exactly what the first secretary wanted to hear about, but the general meaning of Enrique's speech was in line with what Pedro had said and he responded.

PEDRO: We are struggling with that. And we also want the technicians, the engineers, the brigade chiefs to be as much as possible with the people in the coffee plantations, to be where the people are. The bosses are supposed to be there with the workers.
ENRIQUE: Correct!
PEDRO: Why do you think that the brigade of Pepito is the leading one in the construction of the highway and the bridges? Because Pepito is there with his men. Another brigade that worked with the bridges was not so good, but Pepitos's brigade is good, because the first one to work is Pepito. So the example of the boss and the technician is important, Pedro continues, optimistically. I think that we are now at a crucial moment for the revolution, and I think that in the hands of the agricultural workers this big responsibility, that we have to find solutions to the problems, principally with the food, will be met.

Pedro then made a symbolically important reference to himself and the history of the region.

> Before the revolution, practically no goods entered these mountains from outside. I come from here. There were two or three small shops here and they sold cod and some other things, some rice, but the people here survived. And then there was not much less population than now, because most of those who are down here now came from up there. These mountains were really populated; everywhere lots of people were living. . . . But there did not come all the goods that come today. And people lived. People lived, fifty-nine years almost of this century, self-supporting and eating what the soil produced, the pig, the hen, here in the mountains; the peasants produced even rice for their own consumption. They also produced potatoes for subsistence. All that has disappeared. We have to recreate it, because the fundamental thing is, compañeros, our food. With the transportation and the food distribution that we have now, the people don't understand that and they complain a little.

Cuba's history is often referred to when leaders want to emphasize a point, but it is quite rare to allude to it as Pedro did here. Usually leaders recall the *bad* times, the problems, the oppression. Here Pedro emphasized the strength of the people in difficult situations in the past and implicitly criticized the people for being too slack, for not making enough effort. He went on to talk about the rationing, which had increased, and compared it with the situation in the 1970s, when it was much worse. He then talked about socialism in general, a common topic, especially in view of the events in Eastern Europe.

> This situation which has come up, we do not want it like this, but the world is going through a special moment and compared to other Latin American countries and the Third World, our situation is better in many ways. And here we care about the situation of everyone. If we did not have the socialist system that we have, it would be easier to resolve the problems. It is easy to solve them; you just have to do what they did with gasoline [in capitalist countries], raise the price per liter. And he who can, buys. We could take away the libreta and raise the price of meat, rice, eggs, and everything that we distribute. We could raise the prices, and the work centers could fire people. And they

would survive as best they can. That is easy. What is difficult is to guarantee that no one must be out on the street, as Fidel says. Guarantee the food, the transport, guarantee that all of us have the basic food to survive. I think that what is distributed is enough. . . . [10]

We want to congratulate the compañeros on this day, and we want to say that you are not alone in this struggle, the president [of the Poder Popular] and I are also agriculturalists. We congratulate with all our hearts the compañeros who have received medals for their twenty-five years of service in this very difficult sector. You all should bask in the recognition and confidence of the government and the Party. This period now will be a period that will teach everyone to struggle, to be more revolutionary, to rescue socialism and la patria, which so many Cubans have saved in difficult times before. Thank you, and congratulations! [Applause].

¡Patria o Muerte! ¡Venceremos! ¡Viva Fidel! ¡Viva!

Well, you made me speak! [Laughs].

References to socialism and the revolution are made constantly to underscore the good that the state and the Party have brought to the people. Pedro tried to explain what he saw as the core of socialism—the guarantee that *everyone* will have enough to survive. He used the example of capitalist countries to emphasize that in a similar situation people there would starve.

This speech is a good example of both the form and the content of political rhetoric in Cuba. Naturally, it was colored by the situation, the person talking, and the times, but it still follows the general outline of most Cuban political speeches. Local speeches focus mostly on topics that are nationally defined and then tie them to the local situation, as in this speech, in which Pedro talked at length about the Food Program in the municipality. Speeches at the national level are often more ideological and general in content, but the form is very similar. A few days before this speech, Fidel talked in Havana on the thirtieth anniversary of the Committees for the Defense of the Revolution. Like Pedro, he talked about the Food Program, but at the national level. He also talked about the importance of morality and the honor of the people in this difficult situation. Pedro used almost the same words as Fidel did when he talked about rescuing the country. Fidel said, "First of all, we have to rescue the homeland,

[10]Here Pedro speaks about the impossibility of total equality quoted, earlier.

because we want a free and independent homeland, today more than ever." He also coined a phrase that was used rhetorically many times later in Palmera: *¡Gusano, a tu hueco!* "In difficult times, *la gusanera* [the traitors] raise their heads; they must be fought, and we must say to them, "¡Gusano, a tu hueco!" (Worm, back to your hole!). The word *gusano* has been used since 1959 to refer to counterrevolutionaries.

Local leaders who can do so use Fidel's oratory style. They speak without scripts and use the conversational tone that has become so characteristic of Castro. In Pedro's speech, there was real dialogue, but usually the dialogue is rhetorical. The speaker draws the audience into the speech by asking a question that can be answered with a "yes" or a "no" or with a slogan (cf. Paine 1981:17). Pedro's speech both gives information and relays an ideological message. By using many examples from the local arena, Pedro made the members of his audience feel that he was not teaching them but sharing experiences with them. In other contexts, the leaders are not afraid to lead and express their ideas, criticisms, and encouragement forcefully.

Pedro used the pronoun "we" in two different ways in his speech. On the one hand, he used it when he talked about the leaders, including himself, as being the highest authorities in the municipality, something all those present knew. In this way he legitimized his right to define problems and make demands. On the other hand, he included himself in "the people" and indeed "the workers," thereby emphasizing the leaders' unity with the masses and reinforcing his humility and belief in egalitarianism.

Since there is only one Party in Cuba, the leaders do not have to compete with other parties when persuading people of the superiority of socialist ideas (Paine 1981). They do need to be persuasive, however, to get people to accept the legitimacy of the system or to convince people to go along with the goals presented by the leaders. Since no alternative interpretations are officially available, the only options are for people to accept the Party's interpretation of the world or to reject it. People are constantly presented with a view of the world that is conducive to the goals of socialism. Important political issues are brought up in a variety of situations, on TV, in speeches, and in daily activities. This might make acceptance of them likely, but, as we shall see, it can also lead to resentment. The criticism politicians in pluralistic societies freely bestow on other parties is reserved in Cuba for external enemies and the capitalist world, especially the United States.

The Negative Example

In Cuba the enemy is clear, close, and powerful, looming only ninety miles from the northern coast. Cubans recognized that the threat from the United States was real in 1961 after the unsuccessful Bay of Pigs invasion. There have been other attempts to invade, and bombing from U.S. planes occurred even during the 1970s. Since then the feeling of threat has fluctuated, lessening during the Carter presidency and increasing when Reagan and Bush were in power.

Cuba has built a military force that is both large and strong and that also has important symbolic value to the people. All Cubans are part of the militia, training in their special tasks each month on the Día de la Defensa. Quite often there are also special exercises, such as blackouts, in which every citizen is supposed to take part. Such exercises are constant reminders of the possibility of attack. That many Cubans fought in the 1950s during the revolutionary war and that many Cubans have gone on international military missions mean that many people have direct experience with military struggle. Cubans are frightened of war but feel that they can protect themselves should it occur. Patriotism is often expressed in militant ways, by people saying that they will fight to their last drop of blood for Cuba or that the United States will have to destroy all and everything to conquer Cuba.

Militantes as well as the mass media frequently criticize capitalism, with the favorite example of its negative features being the United States. There is a love/hate relationship with the United States, grounded in the long relationship between the two countries. The United States is the principal threat to Cuba, but in a way it is also the standard by which Cuba assesses itself, as Julie Feinsilver (1989) points out in her article about medical care in Cuba. When Cuba's low infant mortality rate is mentioned in Palmera, for example, it is almost always compared with the U.S. figures. Cuban newspapers feature articles about social misery in the United States—how racism, drug abuse, and unemployment result in horrible life situations.

Since all media in Cuba are controlled by the Party, people receive a thorough knowledge of some issues but no knowledge of others. The image presented of other countries and of capitalism often becomes distorted. Capitalism is described in its most crude form, and other forms of capitalism are seldom mentioned. When I talked about capitalism in Sweden, with its strong safety net of social programs, many militantes did not believe me. Fortunately, Fidel alluded to them in a speech, which helped me convince my friends of the special kind of Swedish capitalism.

There is another problem that results because the picture of the capitalist world is so distorted. Many Cubans who are critical of their own system reject their government's image of the United States and then create an equally distorted picture. Their image is constructed from rumors, from letters from people who have moved to the U.S., from American films shown on TV and in cinemas,[11] and from Radio Martí. These people like to believe that life in the United States is fantastic, that it is possible to make a lot of money quickly, and that everyone there lives well. The stubborn refusal of the leaders and the militantes to see anything good in capitalist countries only strengthens these people's idealized views.

Uncompromising rhetoric is also used at times to describe the positive side of Cuba. Leaders may say, for example, that nowhere else in the world do all children have access to free education. That this is simply not true is easy to establish, and the exaggeration can backlash. It has become more and more difficult for the Party to demonstrate the superiority of socialism since the fall of the regimes in Eastern Europe. In addition, after thirty years Cubans have come to accept their relatively good standard of living as natural and some blame socialism for the severe economic problems in the Cuban economy of late.

[11]Although all cultural institutions must adhere to the official ideological line, both cinemas and television show many popular North American films. One of the most popular films at the cinema in Palmera during my fieldwork was *Jaws*.

Criticism

There are several ways for people in Palmera to voice their criticism of Cuban society. Much is said between the lines, and a thorough knowledge of Cuban culture and Cuban Spanish is necessary to understand this criticism. People are surprisingly outspoken in private, however, although my position as a foreigner with good relations to their leaders made some people cautious, especially those whom I did not know well. There are also many degrees of criticism; some Cubans wish for better conditions within the system while others reject it wholesale. Most of the people who are disappointed and disagree with the ideas of socialism lived rather good lives before the revolution and feel that they have lost something. Pérez, an old man who was a local businessman before the revolution, is very critical and disappointed by the way the revolution has developed. He says that "they" took away his shop and his business without paying for it. Now he receives a pension from the state, but he says it is so small that he cannot live on it. Pérez feels bitter because he helped the rebels during the revolutionary war but that they showed no gratitude when they came to power. He feels that Cuban society today is much more brutal and difficult than before. As he sees it, the revolution has not succeeded in making the society better.

Blanca, a woman who grew up on a farm and had a pleasant and comfortable childhood, says that nothing is better now. For her, everything has changed for the worse. She feels that people are more selfish now and no one helps those who have troubles. She says: "Life for most people is worse now than before. Now you could die struggling. No one wants to help you like before. Life has treated me very harshly, very harshly. Today, when you have something, you count with people, but when you do not, they look over your shoulder. There are many hypocrites, too many. Instead of helping you, they try to destroy you." Blanca has a job in which she earns a very low salary, and she feels that she is treated badly because she is poor. She has tried several times to get the government to make repairs on her house, but no one has helped her. She feels that the leaders have not only failed in their job but have behaved in an undignified manner. "It is possible that I do not have a very high nivel, but I have a little more dignity than they have."

Both Pérez and Blanca are bitter about their situations. They feel that the nice words that the political leaders use when talking about the revolution misrepresent reality. For Pérez and Blanca, there has been no improvement. On the contrary, their lives are worse now than before.

One way Palmerans express dissatisfaction is by complaining about their political leaders. Harsh criticism is often delivered at local political meetings, for example. The leadership encourages criticism if it is made openly, on appropriate occasions, and is based on concrete examples. The criticism expressed by those who object to the whole system has none of these characteristics. Instead, it is often vague, mentioned en passant, and implies that the leaders do nothing for the people, that they misuse their power, and that they have too many privileges. This is certainly true in some circumstances, and during the Ochoa trial,[12] several high-ranking political leaders were exposed as corrupt and abusing their power. Local leaders, however, have few opportunities to gain privately from their positions, except in rather marginal ways, but to someone who is already disappointed with the leaders and the system, any flaw seems inexcusable.

Lola had tried for a long time to find a place to live and had not succeeded. She felt unjustly treated by her boss and also by the political leaders in the municipality, who could not or did not want to help her. She remarked bitterly several times that "if I had been a dirigente, I would have had a house five years ago."

Another family had a problem with the water supply in their small house. Family members had complained time and time again to their CDR, the Poder Popular, and the Party but had never gotten results. They could not get hold of the material to fix the problem themselves but were promised that the government would do

[12]In the summer of 1989, a group of high-ranking employees at MININT, the Department of the Interior, were tried and sentenced to death or imprisonment for drug trafficking and corruption. The head of the group was General Armando Ochoa, a former hero of the revolution. The trials were televised, and a big debate on corruption took place, both in the media and among ordinary people (see *Vindicación de Cuba* 1989 and, for another view of the matter, Oppenheimer 1992).

something about it. This situation so much aggrieved the father in the family, who was already doubtful of the system, that he said that he could not go to the meeting with his delegate of the Poder Popular because he felt that the delegate had cheated and abused the family for so long "and I would just make a fool of myself at the meeting." He was also very bitter toward the president of the Poder Popular, whom he had known for many years, and one time said that he "hated the old fart." His reluctance to accept the system, which the political leaders most certainly knew about, might have brought him less favorable treatment, which consequently led to even greater frustration on his part.

Complaints about the constant lack of goods, the poor organization of services, and the sometimes bloated bureaucracy are often heard among people in Palmera. These complaints can be interpreted in several ways. Partly, they can be taken at face value, as evidence that parts of the system do not work. But they can also be seen as implicit protests against the system itself. At times it is difficult to know which is the case.

Pancho, an old farmer who worked as an agricultural worker, was once complaining to his workmates and a man from the local union about the lack of consumer goods. "It's getting worse and worse," he said. "Now there are no shoes at all in the shops, and the only shoes I have are these," he said, showing his heavy, worn boots. "Before we did not want to buy *botas russas* (Russian boots) because they were so badly made, but now I would gladly buy them if there were any. It is terrible, this. I have to have shoes. I could go to work without trousers," he said laughing, "but not without shoes. That is impossible. And there are no files or machetes either. How can we work?" After complaining for a long time, he added: "But even if these are hard times, at least we have enough to eat and all of us have the same. Antes, under capitalism, only those who had money could buy things." This could be taken literally as a complaint about the lack of shoes, files, and machetes, which I think it was in this case, but it could also be seen as a more profound criticism of socialism, with the reference to the past thrown in as a rhetorical safety measure. The only way to assess the meaning is to gain a close knowledge of the person who is speaking.

The Past in the Present

In Cuban society today there is a preoccupation with *before* and after. Whether the point of departure is 1 January, 1959, the victory of the revolution, or 1956, when the struggles began in the Sierra Maestra, antes is seen as a qualitatively different phase in the country's history. The word *antes* carries a whole set of references. Usually this time is seen as an oppressive, cruel, and impoverished period in recent Cuban history, but some view it as a time of opportunities and abundance. Antes has become the metaphor for either the good or the bad life, often portrayed in stark ways, without nuances. Talking about old times is often a way to comment on and to illustrate one's feelings about the present.

Both young and old have a very close relationship to the past. But many older people who have experienced the bad times of antes would agree with Eutimio, an old militante and retired agricultural worker, who said: "Today many of the young people are revolutionaries, but they do not have any profound knowledge about how it was before. They have never had a hard life. To feel poverty and oppression in your flesh *(sufrirlo en su carne)*, that is something else."

When leaders and others talk about life antes, certain topics are brought up more often than others. One of these topics is the poverty that many people in the Palmera region had to endure.[13]

Up to thirty years ago, Palmera was an isolated mountain region with few roads. People lived in small settlements or in a few larger villages, mainly in the mountains. They subsisted on their crops—yucca, plantains, sweet potatoes, yams—and sold some coffee. They kept pigs and goats for the meat. A few big landowners owned most of the land and had people working for them as *jornaleros* (day laborers) or tenant farmers. Other residents worked as charcoal-makers or woodmen, cutting the wood growing mainly on the mountain slopes.

For a short period, there had been a mine in the region operated by a North American company. And then, some decades before the revolution, a North American couple settled in Limones and built a

[13]For an interesting and ample description of life in rural Cuba before the revolution, see Nelson 1950.

big, beautiful house with two stories. The husband owned almost all the land in the vicinity of the town, exploiting it through forestry and cattle raising. The wife had an enormous coffee plantation surrounding a village in the mountains above Limones. In those years, during the 1940s and 1950s, many people living around Limones were employed by los Americanos, as they are still called. At the end of the 1950s, when the threat of victory for the rebels was imminent, the American couple left all their property and went back to the United States.

In the 1920s and 1930s, many people came to this region and started clearing and cultivating land. They usually did not have deeds to their holdings, and the big landowners could easily force them to give up the land or to become tenant farmers. While those were hard years for the poor peasants and jornaleros in the region, in the 1950s the *guardias* (soldiers) of President Batista undertook an even more brutal regime.

Eutimio's story is typical:

> I was born in 1926 in a small village on the coast here in what is now Palmera.[14] My family was *totalmente pobre* [totally poor]. My father was a jornalero and a fisherman. We did not have any land and no animals. We were twelve siblings *de padre y madre* (by father and mother) and seventeen *de padre* (by my father).[15] All the children had to help the family by doing different chores for the local farmers. I started to work as a cowhand when I was thirteen years old. Although I was a child, I remember that it was terribly bad for people here during what we called the *machadato*, the period when Machado was president in the 1930s and 1940s. People hardly ate anything but maize flour. Many died of hunger. There was much violence also. The *guardia rural* [the rural military] could kill anyone as they liked. Later, during Batista, there was also a lot of violence and corruption. The latifundistas paid the guardias so that they would do them favors. Some had them as private bodyguards. The *guardias* helped them drive off peasants who were tending the land on "their" fincas. They even killed

[14]Up to 1976, when a new administrative and political organization was introduced in Cuba, Palmera was not an autonomous municipality but belonged to a larger region.

[15]Since Cubans for many decades have had several partners during their lifetimes, most people describe their siblings as "de padre y madre" or only "de padre."

> those who protested. *Abusar a los pobres* [abuse the poor], that was what they did.

This isolated region, which up to the 1960s could be reached only by boat or by jeep or truck, had almost no doctors and nurses. To get medical care at a hospital, people had to go to the big city, seventy-two kilometers away by boat. Many did not make it. This is evident from the many cemeteries on the coast, which are often pointed out to those who visit the municipality today. A few pharmacists could sell medicine to people, but mostly they went for help to the many *curanderos*, who cured with herbal medicine and magic.

Rafael was born in 1910. He recalled the years when he was a young man:

> In the 1920s and 1930s there were very bad times here. Many people starved. I have always worked a lot so we were okay. My wife and I had eight children, but three of them died in infancy. It was like that in those times, you know; there were no doctors here, and no help for the sick. There were three *lanchas* [boats] to the city, but it took a very long time. You arrived the next day. It cost eighty centavos, even for the sick. If the patients did not have eighty centavos, they either died or recovered. We had a *partera* [midwife], *espiritistas* [spiritualists], who gave both advice and medicine, *curanderos* [healers], who were not religious, and *santigueros* [sorcerers], who can take away the bad when someone has put *mal de ojo* [the evil eye] on you.

As late as the 1950s, some 27 percent of Cubans could not read and write (*Cuba, Territorio Libre* 1981). In this area the figure was most certainly higher. According to Lowry Nelson (1950), the figure for the Oriente was 37 percent in 1943. There were few schools, and the quality of the teachers and the teaching was not very high. Those who could afford it hired a teacher, but most parents felt it was more important for their children to work and do chores at home. "I'm illiterate," Rafael said. "I started to work very early and never went to school. There was not any school where we lived, and furthermore my parents did not think that schooling was necessary. During the literacy campaign there were people here for seven months who were supposed to teach us to read and write, but I never learned anything. I had my work and could not take part in education."

Eutimio had a somewhat similar experience: "I did not go to school until 1963, when I was forty-six years old. Then I became a militante in the Party and could go to the Party school. There I concluded five years of schooling, and we also had political training."

Finally, Anita, born in 1947, told me: "The school I went to was very far away from home. We had to walk for hours. And it was not worth it—we did not learn anything there. The teacher never got up from her chair. She was like a queen, giving orders. I did not learn how to read. I was very headstrong then. It was almost like a punishment to go school. It was better to stay home and pull weeds than to go to that school."

There were a few shops in some of the bigger villages, some bars, and at least one ring for cockfights in Limones. Catholicism was the main religion in the region, but Santeria, a syncretic mixture of Catholicism and African religions, was widespread then as it is now.

Stories of the hard times antes are almost always used to emphasize, implicitly or explicitly, the positive traits of today's society. The harsh and brutal regime of Batista and the history of the Palmera region made many of its inhabitants supportive of the rebels' cause. When they came to the Sierra Maestra, peasants and workers soon started to help them and to join their army. It is difficult to know how much people knew about the aims and goals of the rebels, but the miserable life of many of *los humildes* (the humble), as President Batista called them (Pérez 1988), was enough to make them favor political change. The assistance of local people was vital to the rebels in that they provided geographical guidance through the inaccessible mountains and food and supplies (Almeida Bosque 1989).

Eutimio recalled his role in the struggle:

> For every innocent who was killed by Batista's army, forty or fifty people went up to the mountains. In that way Batista himself nourished the revolution. People fought with anything, often machetes, or they stole arms from the Batista army to be able to fight. Many people here helped the rebeldes. We collected eleven thousand pesos, and a young relative of mine—he was only fifteen or sixteen years old—took the money up to Fidel in the mountains. Many families had given money.

I helped the rebeldes by giving them information, and I also stole animals from the finca where I worked as a foreman and gave to the rebels.

Peréz, who was born in 1908, also helped the rebels:

I hid rebeldes in my cellar, and my wife cooked for them. I also gave them weapons when I could get hold of them. I helped them a lot. The Batista army came here and arrested me. They wanted to kill me because they said that I had helped the mau-maus, as they called the rebels. And that was true, of course. They kept me in the *cuartel* [barracks] for two days, but then the local guardias—some of them were okay—pleaded for me so they let me go.

Marcelo, who was born in 1946, remembered the war from the perspective of a young boy:

I met some of the big ones—Fidel, Raúl, Camilo, Celia, and Hart—during the revolutionary war. They came here to my village. They bought food, clothes, and shoes in the shop. That was in 1957. The rebeldes always paid for everything; they never took anything. We used to be guides for the rebels, and once I went with Fidel. There were so many bad Batista soldiers here. One of them called Masferrer was a real murderer. He killed many people, but for every peasant they killed, more and more people wanted to join the rebels. My family helped as much as we could with horses, food, and cooperation. My father was a mule driver, and he was taken prisoner by the Batista army, high up in the mountains. He was a prisoner for four months, and they had him transport things for them with his mules. Sometimes he would tell the Batista army the location of a rebel encampment, but then he had already sent a message with someone to warn them so that they had disappeared when the army came.

After the revolutionary war had been won, Fidel and the other leaders remembered the people in the mountains by instituting many reforms that were especially useful to "the humble ones" in the Sierra. Children from the mountain villages were sent to special schools, roads were built, medical care was made available throughout the country, and land reform gave private farmers the right to hold up to sixty-five hectares of land. The growth of administrative and political centers on the coast attracted many mountain peasants to move there.

For many in the remote countryside in Cuba, especially women and girls, the revolution brought an opportunity for education. This occurred in part through the literacy campaign but also because Fidel arranged to have special schools created for the purposes of educating rural children such as Anita, who was born in 1947:

> My father did not want me to go to school in Havana, but I made an application myself to the Ana Betancourt school for peasant girls. That was a school directly run by the FMC for the education of women. I wanted to be a schoolteacher. I had always wanted that, and I thought that I did not learn anything at school here. We went to Havana by car, boat, and train. I had never been inside a car before, and of course not in a train. After that very tough journey, we came to Havana and they brought us to a house in Miramar that would be our hostel. That was like a dream. That rich house. I remember that we came in and there was beautiful furniture; there was everything, but we sat down on the floor, dead from fatigue. I will never forget that they gave us a little box with white rice and a steak. That was glorious. After that terrible journey. A revolutionary instructor, as they called them, came and took care of us. They gave us a test to determine which class we would go to, and I went to the first grade. But we were twelve, thirteen years old, so they accelerated the education. They taught us everything, everything. It's terrible that I have forgotten so much of what they taught us. They taught theater, dance, choir singing, playing instruments, and the teachers were really good. Every Sunday we went to the cinema or to the aquarium or some other place. We went to see plays, that play of Hamlet, and I did not understand anything then. They wanted to cram all culture into our heads, just like that, in one stroke. The century of ignorance that made us so backward, they wanted to take that away in no time.

These remembrances build on personal experiences of the times antes. The phrasing of these accounts is inspired by the form and content of ideological messages conveyed by the leaders, which often use history to highlight aspects of the present. The experiences, however, are real to the people who related them. Memories like these, I am convinced, are one of the principal reasons so many people continue to support the Cuban revolution.

Rhetoric of Ordinary People

Both leaders and "ordinary people" use political rhetoric situationally. Because of the leaders' role, they use rhetoric whenever they can to spread an ideological message; by contrast, ordinary people seldom use such rhetoric in daily activities. They are more apt to use political rhetoric at meetings or in other formal situations. Often people promise, almost by rate, to do a special quantity of work, as the bridge workers did. This happens at almost all big meetings and is often encouraged by the leaders. No doubt the intent is often to achieve the goal, and at times the promises are fulfilled, but just as often they disappear into thin air. In 1989, all dirigentes promised to pick thirty latas of coffee during the harvest. At the end of the harvest, some of the dirigentes had picked thirty latas, while others had picked only five, six or even fewer. This may have been discussed in the nucleos of the Party, to which I did not have access, but officially nothing was said about the poor result. The reasons for not following up on this and other promises might be that everyone knows that some things that are said are only political rhetoric. Another reason might be that achieving the practical conditions for success (transportation, tools, etc.) is often difficult, so that it is better not to discuss why promises were not kept.

Another common use of rhetoric is to pledge allegiance to the revolution. Gloria, a woman in her thirties who is not a militante and who seldom took part in voluntary work and never talked about politics or expressed herself in ideological terms in our many conversations, said during an interview about her life: "For me, the revolution has been very good. Other countries might have revolutions, but there is none like ours. Like my revolution—none, like my country—none; I'm telling you, like my country—none, and like my leader—none, and *por eso yo muero* [for this I would die]." A while later, she said: "*Chica*, for me the most important thing in my life is the revolution and my family. And within the revolution, my work, my organizations, and all the good things my country has. That's the most important. And our comandante en jefe, that is the most important." I had not introduced the topic of the revolution but had asked her what she thought was most important in her life. Her answer surprised me, and I am still not sure what this political rhetoric meant to her.

Rafael, an old man who had lived a very hard life working as a day laborer, a coal worker, and an agricultural worker, said that "the revolution has made everything 100 percent better." Dora, a black woman who had also grown up in bad conditions, said, "What do you think I would have been without the revolution—nothing."

Emilia was about seventy years old, had worked very hard, had many children to support, and had been very poor before the revolution. She made a spontaneous personal proclamation of her revolutionary values during a meeting of the municipal FMC in Limones. She said that she always tried to give her children two sets of values in life.

> I have borne sixteen children. Five of them died, but I have always worked hard and tried to give the children a good upbringing. It is true that antes, before the revolution, it was hunger that drove me to work, but after the revolution I worked for la patria because I knew that it was necessary. I have worked for the revolution, which has done so many fantastic things for us. I have brought up my children with the following norms: in life—*servir* [serve], *honradez* [honesty], *vergüenza* [shame]—and in the revolution—*trabajo* [work], *sacrificio* [sacrifice], and *lucha* [struggle].

Emilia used many of the catch words of Cuban socialism but also spoke from personal experience. She referred to her role of mother, a very important role for women in Cuba, but also of revolutionary mother, which is almost sacred.

It is, of course, impossible to say what people "mean" in any deep sense when they use revolutionary rhetoric. Some may be trying to make an impression on others, to show that they are good revolutionaries. Gloria does not actively contribute very much to the revolution, but she is loyal to it. She has strong feelings for her country and society. It might be that she took the opportunity to say so in a formal interview in which her words would not sound as grand as they would in everyday conversation. For Emilia and others like her, words and action go hand in hand; these people often express themselves in more personal ways, since they can talk about their own experiences. Then there are those, like the young boy who worked on the bridge (see chap. 3), who, in the words of the first secretary of the province, "do not say much but work all the more."

[6]

The Revolutionary Act

At six in the morning on 8 October 1989, thirty-five other people and I mounted a flatbed truck in the square in Limones to go up to a mountain village to pick coffee. It was dark and cool, and the moon was shining. Men and women from many different workplaces were going out on their free day to do voluntary work. People were joking and bantering. The truck was crowded, and when it was going up an especially steep hill, the motor overheated. A man who stood very close to a young woman shouted: "Oooooh, I can feel the smell of heat!" Everyone laughed. A woman close by me said to her friend that she really did not have time to be doing this. She needed the day to do washing and ironing, but she had so few merits that she felt compelled to go (cf. Rosenthal 1992; Smith and Padula 1988).

After standing on the bumping truck for more than an hour, we came to a farm where a guide showed us each to a *carrera* (a lane of coffee plants) that we were supposed to pick *al hecho* (clean of all coffee berries).[1] I was working next to my friend Carlos, who grew up on a finca and is a very skilled coffee picker. He is not a militante but works as a dirigente in an administrative position. He said that coffee harvesting was the most important voluntary work since it generated desperately needed foreign currency.

It was difficult to pick the berries because the plants grew on a steep hill. They were as high as trees, and lianas and other vegetation

[1]When only ripe berries are picked, it is called *al pulpo*.

were entwined in them. On my other side, Susana was steadily picking. She is an assistant in one of the shops in Limones. We called to each other, joking and encouraging each other. A bit farther away a man was singing a romantic song. When Susana saw some other people sitting down, talking and laughing, she became irritated that they were not doing anything but playing around. "I don't know why they come," she said. Then she shouted at them at the top of her voice: "Come on, do some work and don't just play around." They shouted back that she should mind her own business.

We picked frantically, mostly in silence, filling the baskets or bags we had tied around our waists and later emptying them into bigger sacks. I could see Carlos's strawhat bobbing up and down as he bent and stretched to reach all the berries.

We stopped working in the afternoon at about two o'clock. I was very tired and soaked with sweat, so Carlos carried my sack up to the weighing area. The weigher told me that I had picked 3.5 latas; Carlos had picked 7 latas and Susana 4 latas. We were given food on a tin tray—spaghetti, a little carne rusa, rice, and mashed plantains. We sat down to eat, sweaty and dirty from the spiderwebs, lianas, and sticks in the forest, but content with our work. Others came and joined us, eating and waiting to go home on the truck. Carlos reminded us that it was the anniversary of Che Guevara's death, and all agreed that we could not have honored his memory in a better way.

Jorge Domínguez (1978) describes the Cuban political system as a mobilization system since it is based on the mobilization of the whole people in support of socialist ideas, principally through normative incentives: "Political mobilization educates the masses about the goals and methods of revolutionary policies. . . . Political mobilization is a large-scale political activity, educational, change-oriented, continuous, and often nonelectoral, under the hierarchical direction of the party and the mass organizations" (1978:299). To most Cubans, this mobilization system is manifest in meetings of their union, the FMC, the CDR, and their constituency and in defense activities in the militia and in voluntary work.

These mobilizations, which I have earlier described as "participation" and which are an important part of Cuban socialist democracy, are viewed mostly as revolutionary acts. It is often said that "you don't make a revolution with words, but with actions" (Rosendahl 1992a:80).

The concept of mobilization implies that there is close contact between the leaders and the people. As was noted above, the political leaders spend a lot of time urging, cajoling, motivating, and inspiring people into doing more for the revolution.

Although the leaders and the ideological state apparatus—the Party, mass media, schools, and mass organizations (cf. Althusser 1971)—formulate and spread an ideological message, the leaders emphasize that one's personal experiences are also important in building the revolution. These can include one's experiences of hardship and oppression before the revolution, but also the experience of participating in the construction of the new society today.

This idea was developed principally by Che Guevara, who emphasized that the most efficient means for changing people's attitudes is by involving them in the practical act of building the society. The view that ongoing struggle shapes the revolutionary person is part of this idea. The Party program states that the communist is created in combat (*Programa del PCC* 1987:59). Sometimes "combat" is interpreted literally, as military struggle during the revolution or the international missions made by thousands of Cubans up to 1990. According to Guevara, however, instead of seeing revolutionary acts as referring only to military struggle in a revolutionary war, many different forms of social action were to be defined as revolutionary acts.

The most dramatic and highly prestigious revolutionary acts are going on an international mission and working in a contingente or work group. A contingente is composed of vanguard workers who undertake to do a job in a certain amount of time by working extremely hard, for long hours, and with very little free time. They then obtain extra privileges in the form of food, lodgings, and appreciation by the state. These groups are often used as examples by the leaders when they exhort "ordinary people" to work harder for the revolution. One such "famous" contingente is the Contingente Blas Roca, composed of construction workers. Less dramatic acts include doing a good job at work, taking part in mass organizations, being a delegate at the asamblea, and doing voluntary labor.

There are several different types of "voluntary labor," and they are more or less voluntary. The basic idea is that many people are mobilized to do some necessary or urgent task in their spare time, such as picking coffee during the peak of the season. Sometimes people have to help during ordinary work hours. Then the job is not really voluntary but the work place obliges people to participate. The CDR also organizes voluntary work, such as cleaning the neighborhood. In that voluntary work is part of the emulación socialista (socialist competition), those who want to be chosen as model workers must join voluntary work details to gain the chance to buy goods inexpensively.

Although people often say that there is less enthusiasm for voluntary work then there was in the early years of the revolution, many Cubans still do voluntary work and feel it makes an important contribution to society and the revolution. In Palmera, where coffee is the most important crop bringing in foreign currency, many people go out to pick coffee both on workdays and on free weekends during the coffee harvest.

That people understand voluntary work as a political activity can be seen in the case described above. Although Carlos was not a militante and did not have a leading role in the coffee picking, he reminded us that by doing voluntary work we were honoring Che Guevara. Likewise, in November 1990 the Domingo Rojo (Red Sunday) was to be celebrated to commemorate the Russian Revolution. I had taken part in Domingo Rojos in other years, and at least on this day, the militantes had readily gone out to do voluntary work. In 1990, however, several militantes voiced the opinion that it now seemed unecessary or even ridiculous to do so in view of what was happening in Russia.

Cubans are constantly urged to do more for the revolution, to sacrifice more. At times, they feel tired, irritated, or even disgusted with the leaders and the Party who are the instruments of, and symbolize, these demands. Criticism of the need for mobilizations comes from both men and women, but more often from women. They have very heavy workloads at home in addition to being wage earners and must therefore sacrifice more than men to do voluntary labor.

To many Cubans being an elected representative is not seen as a revolutionary act, yet when leaders urge the people to vote in elections and choose the best candidates, they emphasize that being a delegate to the municipal, the provincial, and national asambleas is an important way to contribute to the revolution. At an asamblea, a provincial leader talked to the delegates and urged them to do better jobs. He then emphasized how important their posts were and that they represented many people. "Everyone in Palmera cannot be here," he said, "and therefore it is so important that you are in tune with what the people want and need. The most important thing is to have good rapport with people so that we can help build the country." Thus, the act of serving in an assembly was elevated to a revolutionary act.

The asamblea municipal

The delegates elected to sit in the asamblea municipal of Palmera come from all over the municipality—from small towns on the coast and from remote mountain villages.[2] They are people with all kinds of occupations—laborers, farmers, teachers, administrators, and politicians. They have differing views on how to run the municipality but are all considered by their fellow citizens to be the best people to represent them. In 1989, there were eighty-one delegates in the asamblea municipal of Palmera, of whom twelve, or 15 percent, were women.[3]

Meetings of the asamblea municipal of Palmera are almost always held in the cinema in Limones. Delegates from all over the municipality come in buses, on horseback, in jeeps, and on foot to take part in the decision making. The women dress up in nice dresses, with their makeup immaculate and their hair beautifully set; the men wear guayabera, the pleated shirt for formal occasions, cowboy hats, and boots, and some even sport spurs. The entrance to the cinema is decorated with the Cuban flag and sometimes also the red and black banner of the Movimiento 26-7. Inside the cinema the lights are low, since electricity is always a problem in Palmera. A podium is erected on the stage, with a rostrum on the side. Almost all the

[2]For a comparative discussion of municipal assemblies, see Bengelsdorf 1994.

[3]In 1988, there were only nine female delegates among the total seventy-nine, or 11 percent. In 1984, the figure for the whole country was also 11 percent (Bengelsdorf 1988:127).

delegates are present, since being a delegate is a very serious obligation and permission to be absent is granted only for important reasons.

The day begins early, with a breakfast of juice and sandwiches outside the cinema for those who have come a long way. Others partake of the drinks and sandwiches to fortify them for what will be at least four or five hours of discussions. A little before 9:00, the delegates are urged to take their seats. The meeting begins with a scratchy tape recording of the national anthem: "Al combate corred, bayameses, que la patria os contempla orgullosa . . ." (Run to the battle, citizens of Bayamo, so that the homeland can be proud of you) they sing very solemnly, the men standing at attention. The secretary of the Poder Popular takes a roll call and mentions those absent and the reasons they are not present.[4]

On the podium sit the president of the Poder Popular, who presides over the meeting, the vice president, the first or second secretary of the Party in Palmera, the secretary of the Poder Popular, who also takes minutes, and perhaps an invited guest.[5] After some formalities, discussion begins on the issues on the agenda, which the delegates have received in advance. People are allowed to speak at length and are seldom interrupted. The president of the Poder Popular urges the delegates to participate. He says that the aim of the asamblea is to analyze problems in depth, and it does not matter if this takes time. When the president feels that people are speaking just for the sake of hearing their own voices, however, he interrupts and orders them to be more specific and brief. The political leaders who are present often join in the discussions, interpreting and putting a more ideological cast on an issue. The issues discussed at the asambleas are matters of principle, affecting the entire municipality.[6] All state companies and organizations regularly render accounts of their activities at the asambleas, and oversight commissions formed by the Poder Popular report on their work.[7]

[4]If someone is absent without an explanation, this is also mentioned.

[5]This description builds on notes from several meetings.

[6]It is specifically mentioned in the guidelines of the Poder Popular that the asamblea must deal with matters that concern the whole municipality.

[7]These commissions monitor the activities of the various state companies and organizations under the jurisdiction of the asamblea.

At a meeting of the asamblea municipal in November 1988, the commission analyzing the work of the transport sector in Palmera gave a very critical report. It said that of forty-eight buses in Palmera, twenty-six were not working because they lacked spare parts. The quality of the repairs was very bad, and workers did not work a full eight-hour day, it said. In this case, as in most others, the recommendations were general and vague. The commission recommended that the transport sector be more productive, use its resources better, end poor discipline at work, utilize the vehicles better, and so on. The head of the transport sector was allowed to answer the allegations. He agreed that there were problems, but said that to a great extent they were all because it was so difficult to acquire parts. He said that the transport sector was working on improving service and repairs.

Everyone in Palmera knew that transportation was a problem and all this had been said many times before. There was little discussion. A man from Limones said that the cars and buses were not being fully used and often one could see them parked here and there. The chief of the commission added that the foremen at work sites had to better control the workers so that they worked longer and more productively. A delegate agreed. The president repeated that the problem was the lack of spare parts. No one else said anything, so the president made a motion, which the asamblea approved, that a study be conducted of the utilization of transport vehicles. By a show of hands, the reports from the transport sector and the commission were accepted.

The issue most discussed in the asambleas was the performance of the agricultural sector. This is the most important sector in the municipality, and, as one man said, almost all people have personal experience with it, either as direct producers, administrators, or consumers.

At the November 1989 asamblea, a delegate from a village outside Limones was very critical of the organization of the agricultural sector. Too much fruit, viandas, and coffee in the countryside were not harvested, he said, and there were many fincas where the coffee had not been picked. He said that he went with some people from his constituency to pick coffee at one of those underharvested fincas, but "we did not get enough help from the leaders. There were several of those who picked coffee who were not paid."[8] Nonetheless, he recommended that other delegates do the same. He also suggested that a method be developed to control the quality of agricultural products.

The president had asked this man at various times during his speech what specifically he wanted to propose. Now the president asked if he wanted to make a motion that work be more efficient. "Yes," said the man, "that is what I want."

Another man continued on the same topic. He said that in one mountain village, a lot of mature coffee berries had fallen to the ground and that the coffee was of the best quality in this municipality. "It is a disgrace," he said, "that the organization has not functioned. It was said [by the authorities] that 120 persons were mobilized to pick coffee and only *nine* came. We have to organize this better," the man emphasized. Another man agreed that the EMA (the agricultural company) should organize its work more efficiently. It did not use all of its technicians, he said. Another man added that people needed to be mobilized to the mountains year-round, not only during the coffee harvest.

The president said, "Now you are saying what other people have already said." Undisturbed, the man added that there was also a lot of stealing going on during coffee harvesting: "There is much coffee that does not get to the drying places. Many people have sacks of coffee at home and do not deliver it to the EMA. And people are very undisciplined. Once a driver was ordered to go to El Pico, very high up in the mountains, but he did not want to go, so he went instead to Campo Abajo, which is much more accessible. That cannot be allowed!" A representative from the EMA said that the workers had been more productive than the previous year. In El Pico, for example, the harvest was one-thousand latas the previous year and more than eight thousand *latas* that year.[9]

The criticism with respect to the inefficiency, negligence, and

[8]During the coffee harvest, people who go on voluntary work parties to pick coffee are paid a small sum for each lata they pick. When they work on a workday, the money usually goes to their workplace or to the organization they go with, such as their CDR.

[9]One lata is approximately twenty liters.

poor organization of the agricultural sector was serious. Yet the discussion did not lead to any real proposals for change. The harsh criticism by the man who said that coffee was not picked on many fincas was reformulated by the president into a rather harmless suggestion that the coffee be harvested more efficiently. This discussion has occurred many, many times, and although the criticism may be harsh, few concrete measures are taken to improve the situation. As in the transport sector, the problems are so enormous that everyone knows they are very difficult to solve. Still the delegates keep on criticizing, and sometimes the criticism leads to change when the Party and the government instigate it. The results, however, do not come directly from suggestions at the asamblea, which functions more as a place for discussion and the exchange of opinions (cf Moore 1977:152).

During the five asambleas that I attended, no one voted against or entered an objection to the majority decision in the minutes. When I asked if anyone ever objected, a professional in the Poder Popular said that it had happened but very seldom. His explanation was that matters were discussed so thoroughly that everyone knew that the decisions made were sensible ones. Many times the delegates have a preparatory seminar, as it is called, at which the leaders from the Poder Popular and the Party explain matters to the delegates. (I never took part in any of these meetings.)

The fact that no one votes against any decisions is indicative of the authority and the power that the Party and the professionals in the Poder Popular have over the delegates. When the first or second secretary of the Party explains that things cannot or ought not to be done right now or ever, almost everyone accepts this assessment. Some try to discuss it and present contradictory opinions, but when it comes to voting, decisions are almost always made unanimously (cf. Jørgensen 1983:36). At times I have seen a meeting of the asamblea as a Greek drama in which everyone has his or her given place and role. This is in line with David Kideckel's account (1983) of collective-farm delegate assemblies in Romania but somewhat different from Sally Falk Moore's discussion of Tanzania (1977). Moore argues that the aim of the local assembly is to show the unanimity of the participants. I contend that the aim of the Palmeran asambleas is to provide a forum for disagreement and criticism in a context that can be both controlled and shaped by the highest leaders.[10] Certain complaints and suggestions *are* attended to by the Party and by the Poder Popular, but only at their discretion. The delegates may and do take initiatives, but the Party and the officials of the Poder Popular set the limits on how these initiatives should be treated.

There are several possible explanations for this. First, the leaders have a wider knowledge of the political and economic situation in the municipality and therefore make other judgments than the delegates, who often are biased by their own experiences from one part of the municipality. Secondly, the leaders are limited by the decisions and framework that the higher governing levels impose on the municipality. Third, given Cuba's centralist structure of decision making, the delegates know that the leaders usually have the last word and find it futile to protest. Little in the way of explanation is needed when a decision made at the municipal level is reversed at a higher level. Most delegates verbally express an understanding of the point of view of the leaders but also complain sometimes about the capriciousness of decision making.

Resistance through Indifference and Withdrawal

From the point of view of the leaders and those who want to be seen as good revolutionaries, a good revolutionary is one who *acts*. Accordingly, the easiest form of protest is to show indifference to or to withdraw from political activities. A person can thus protest without actually voicing any disagreement out loud. Withdrawal and indifference occur in many political systems and are usually interpreted as evidence of a lack of interest in politics. In Cuba, however, verbally protesting against the system can be interpreted as counterrevolutionary. Frequent indifference and withdrawal, which compared with what occurs in other countries might seem like no protest at all, must be understood to be a subtle and relatively safe measure of very real protest in Cuba. As one person, who did not want to but felt

[10] The procedure for voting is that the president asks: "Those in favor raise their hands." Then: "Anyone against?" and finally: "Anyone abstaining?"

obliged to go to a meeting, put it, "I really hope it rains tonight so that the wretched meeting is canceled."

One way to protest is by failing to pay membership dues to mass organizations by claiming lack of money. Sitting on the porch at a friend's house, we saw the treasurer of the CDR come to collect the annual membership fee (three pesos). My friend hissed, "Here he comes again—*begging*!" Not paying, however, is very obvious since the fees are not high and it is difficult to claim that one cannot afford them.

Another way to protest is by not participating in meetings. This can be done by going away, or claiming to be ill. Or, if one cannot avoid attending the meeting, one can avoid saying anything. Privately, those who feel forced to take part in mass organizations complain that the leaders do not accomplish anything and that the organizations have become goals in themselves and ask for money all the time. Repeated avoidance of meetings is, of course, interpreted by others as evidence of a negative attitude toward the system.

Voluntary work is another activity through which Cubans can express disinterest. Some claim to be sick or find other reasons not to participate. Others do voluntary work but avoid working very hard. They sit and smoke, sneak away and do other things, pick fruits and vegetables for themselves, chat with others, and so forth. This leads to conflicts with others who have come to work, and to work hard, and who get irritated seeing some people loaf (Rosendahl 1992a). Those who oppose voluntary work often declare that it is a waste of time because the work is not worth the effort and the people who do it at times ruin more than they produce. This is certainly true of some voluntary work, in construction, for example, where people are put to work doing tasks they do not know how to do. At a voluntary work party to build a school in Palmera, my work group was instructed to repaint hundreds of sheets of roofing that another group of voluntary workers had painted incorrectly a few days before. During the coffee harvest, the voluntary workers accomplished much, however, although they did not work as fast as skilled agricultural workers. Many rationalizations of the futility of voluntary labor are thus excuses, and what they are really expressing is a negative attitude toward the political system.

Social Control

The protest element in withdrawing and expressing indifference is underscored by the fact that it is very difficult in Cuba to deviate in any way whatsoever, either by not participating in activities or by behaving in an oppositional manner.

The Cuban system is often called totalitarian and repressive. I would describe the Palmeran system as marked by strong social control. In Palmera, the communities are small, people are open and communicative, and most people know one another personally and can therefore keep track of one another easily. As noted earlier, in the elections for example, pioneros are sent out to bring those who have not voted to the polling stations.

When the CDR in the multifamily building where I lived was going to meet, the general secretary went around to all the apartments a few days beforehand to tell people or to leave a note with the time and date of the meeting. Those who could not come were supposed to notify the executive committee and state their reason. On the night of the meeting, members of the executive committee were always present at the site of the meeting, before everyone else. By a quarter of an hour or so after the scheduled meeting time, when few residents had yet come downstairs, the committee members started to shout to the open balconies and windows, "Hey, you, compañeros, MEETING!" Some of my neighbors put their heads out and said that they were coming, but others tried to pretend that they were not at home. After a while more, the committee members started to become more personal: "Rosita," someone shouted, "get your ass out here!" "Pedro, where are you?" "I've showered," Pedro answered. "I have to put some clothes on." "Never mind," the woman on the ground shouted, "come as you are, *we* don't mind!" Everyone laughed. The bantering is good-natured, but for those who really do not want to attend, it is a difficult situation. The effect is cumulative. Those who feel forced to attend a meeting or to do voluntary work become even more negative toward the mass organizations and the Party. This leads to resistance, to pressure from the leaders, to more resistance, to more pressure, and so on.

The local units of the mass organizations have the explicit task of controlling antisocial behavior. From the beginning the CDR was a militant guard unit, meant to protect Cuban society and communities from counterrevolutionary actions and infiltration by its enemies (Brenner et al. 1989; Butterworth 1974; Domínguez 1978). Today the CDR has a more social role and its members care for the order and beauty of their neighborhoods. Social control, however, is still an important task. Cederistas, as they are called, are supposed to keep an eye on outsiders who come to a barrio or village, and to try to prevent antisocial behavior. This can mean petty vandalism by schoolchildren, drunkenness, and politically suspicious behavior, but also objectionable personal behavior. Representatives from the FMC and the CDR, for example, visit families who have problems with alcoholism or spousal abuse.

At a meeting of the FMC, the women talked about a family in which the man was an alcoholic. He was a good man, one woman said, and a militante, but he drank a lot, and when he drank he was terrible—a nuisance for the barrio and very unpleasant to his children. The members of the FMC decided to form a committee of three women who would visit the man and talk to him. One woman was elected to the committee because she was tough, the others said. The man's wife was present, and the chairwoman asked her if it was acceptable to her that they talk to him. She agreed but did not seem to think it would help.

On other occasions discussions at a meeting can lead to intervention in someone's affairs. At a CDR meeting, Elena, who lived on the bottom floor of my building, brought up a problem that had annoyed her for some time. There were canisters of gas that belonged to neighbors who lived upstairs just outside her balcony, and she was worried about her safety. She also complained about the mess that was created when rain bounced off the canisters onto her balcony, bringing mud and dirt. She was furious when talking about this and would not listen to the others, who tried to explain that the gas company had placed the canisters near her balcony and that they could not be moved by anyone except someone from the company. She could not be calmed, not even when a man promised to go see someone at the company and ask to have the canisters moved. "You don't care about me," she shouted. "No one cares that I have to clean and clean all the time. That does not matter to those of you who do not live down here. I'm the slave here," she shouted. "I'm the slave here."

Several people told Elena to calm down and that they would try to solve the problem. The discussion shifted to other matters, but in the end Ana, another neighbor, brought up the matter of the canisters again. She said that she thought that Elena had behaved very inappropriately. "She has a right to say what she thinks; everyone has," Ana said, but to shout and to express herself as Elena had was inexcusable. "Especially since she did it in front of Mona," Ana said, "who is a guest from another country, and in front of the children. How will they know how to behave when they see examples like these." Others agreed, but again Elena stated loudly that no one understood her. The meeting dissolved into chaos. The chairwoman of the CDR later came up to me and said that she agreed with Ana and that she would talk to Elena about the matter. This very personal and individual problem had been made into a public issue. In this case, the social control function of the committee had taken on an educational and moralistic component. The collectivity had demanded that its members behave in a dignified way.

Some people do not agree that such moral judgments should be made publicly. When problem families were discussed at a FMC meeting in a coastal village, for example, a woman said that she thought it was wrong to judge people publicly. Most of the time these reprimands have little effect in solving the concrete problem, but they are a check on people's behavior.

To Fulfill and Sacrifice

The idea of the revolutionary act is rife with moral connotations. The two words used to describe the duty of militantes and others to do whatever they can for the society and the revolution are the verbs *cumplir* (to carry out, fulfill) and *sacrificarse* (to sacrifice). People are expected to carry out and fulfill their promises and to take responsibility for the development and perfection of the revolution and socialism. Implicit in the wider notion that one should do one's best for every task that the revolution demands, is also a sacrifice. Every good revolutionary must sacrifice whatever is necessary and to do so willingly. In fact, sacrifice is seen as something commendable in itself. The statues of the Party say that the militante must "act with a spirit of self-denial and sacrifice, adhering without limits to the revolutionary cause of the proletariat, and be ready to offer for her [the revolution] even his or her life, should it be necessary" (*Estatutos del PCC* 1986:4). Sacrifice is thus a means of creating the new revolutionary person. To sacrifice requires expending time, effort, and strength to build the new revolutionary society. This can be done by being disciplined and doing voluntary work, but also by attending meetings to receive information or to make decisions. It includes surviving with minimal consumer goods and enduring the difficulties that the country is going through, especially now, all without complaining.

Cuban citizens are taught from a very young age to do everything they are asked to do for their society. Smaller children tend gardens at school and help clean up the school yard; older children do manual work collectively, and from the age of six when they start school children are members of the Pioneer movement. Through these activities, they learn to work in mass organizations, but they also learn the normative language of the revolution. Work groups and individuals are encouraged to set goals for their work, for example, to promise to fulfill a specific amount of work by a certain date or to make their workplace a *modelo*. When these goals are reached, the Party and sometimes the Poder Popular recognize the sacrifice by giving out medals or other awards, most of which are nonmaterial.

An element of sacrifice is also built into the rhetoric of socialist competition. In competing to be the best workers, and the most diligent and loyal to their workplaces and workmates, people, of course, are hoping they will have the opportunity to buy household items at prices well below those on the open market or to get a car or better housing. In the ideological representation of socialist competition, however, the aspect of sacrifice to the society and the revolution is more important. People are expected to work hard and to help further the cause of the revolution, and in so doing they may also gain something personally. This is underlined by the fact that *dirigentes* do not take part in the competition. They have some privileges already, in housing for example, but the most important reason the leaders do not participate is ideological. Political leaders at the municipal level are often the people who work the hardest, have the most responsibility, and really do sacrifice the most.

Militantes are totally subordinate to the orders of the Party. They are expected to carry out and sacrifice more than others because they are expected to be examples to others. They are, for example, obliged to take any post or to do any task the Party assigns to them unless they have very special reasons for not doing so. If the Party leaders feel that a militante can do a good job in a post, most militantes say, he will accept it. There are, of course, prestige and status connected to the higher leadership posts in politics and state companies. None of the people who fill these posts ever mention these privileges, however. Instead, they all describe their elevation to higher positions in ideologically "correct" ways. A militante who has worked in many different posts proudly said: "I have never asked for any job. The Party has sent me to these jobs and I am happy to cumplir."

The Ultimate Sacrifice

Most of the sacrifices Cubans have made have been rather undramatic, but, until 1991, there was one sacrifice that could very well mean death (cf. Valdés 1992:221–23). Every militante could be selected or volunteer to do international missions.[11] These could be medical or educational missions abroad or military missions like those to Ethiopia and Angola. The missions were mostly for two years but could be longer. Going on a mission gave merits to the militante in his "private life," at work, for example, and, of course, also resulted in merits politically. The matter was formulated, however, in an ideological way as a patriotic and revolutionary act (see Rosendahl 1992a). Many militantes participated in missions because, as they expressed it, they wanted to bring the advantages of Cuban society to countries less fortunate than Cuba. In light of the oppression of other peoples, the way of life in Cuba seemed to many to be a very good life. *Internacionalistas* whom I met in Palmera said that they wanted to help free the Angolan people, who were threatened by imperialist forces. Some internacionalistas who had been in combat

[11]In 1991, Cuba stopped sending people on international military missions.

were obviously shocked by what they experienced and did not want to talk much about it. Others clearly were proud of their achievements.

Many people who had not been on missions seemed to agree with the official ideology that it was good for Cuba to have internacionalistas in other countries. It has become an issue in which most people share patriotic pride.

To the Party, creating and sustaining a feeling of unity around its main ideas is very important. This sense of togetherness and unity is expressed against mutual enemies and in mutually shared experiences. The ceremony I will describe here illustrates how ritual is used to enhance both the feeling of unity and the normative importance of the idiom of sacrifice.

The seventh of December 1989 was a day of mourning for all of Cuba. On that day, all the internacionalistas who had been killed doing military or social missions in other countries were buried. Solemn funeral ceremonies were held throughout Cuba to honor the memory of the dead men and women. Finally, it was possible to repatriate the corpses from Angola, and only now could families bury their loved ones who may have died several years before.

There was a prohibition on selling alcoholic beverages from 6:00 P.M. on the day before the burials until 12:00 P.M. of the day itself. No one wanted to risk any disturbance or scandal during the event. Days before, my friends with jobs in the municipal office had gone about arranging for the band, loudspeakers, security, medical care, transportation, and many other details.

The families of the four men to be buried in Palmera gathered on the night of 6 December at a wake to honor their dead. Some people had known for several years that their relatives were dead but still felt this was a genuine funeral since they had not been able to bury them when they died. Each family was accompanied by a doctor and a nurse and by a Party member. Paco, a Party member who had done missions in both Ethiopia and Angola and seen several friends die and been wounded himself, said that the wake was difficult both for him and the families. The medical staff gave people sedatives and cared for the families so that they could continue through the day of the burial.

Early on the morning of the funeral, people traveled in buses, trucks, cars, and on foot toward the village where the funeral was being held. Thousands of people were milling about in the vicinity of the ceremony site, and some were standing in line in a small house where the two caskets and the two boxes of bones had been placed and the families were seated. The caskets and boxes were surrounded by flowers, and each casket had a photo of the deceased and the Cuban flag on top. Every third minute a new honor guard, composed of four young militia men and women clad in the militia uniform—beret, white gloves, black armbands, and rifles with mourning crepe—marched in high steps in and out in slow motion. All of the officials at the ceremony were also dressed in military uniform.

It was silent, which is unusual at public events in Cuba. People spoke in low voices as they watched the changing of the guards and waited to file by the dead to pay their last respects.

At 3:30 in the afternoon, the climax of the ceremony began. Representatives of different military and paramilitary units (army, navy, coast guard, MININT) formed an honor guard. Some old fighters from the revolutionary struggle in the mountains stood guard, solemn and heartfelt expressions on their faces. Melba Hernández, one of the female heroes from the revolutionary war visiting from Havana, also stood guard, as did the four top politicians of Palmera—the president and the vice president of the Poder Popular and the first and second secretaries of the Party. The flowers, two caskets, and two boxes were carried out and put in cars and on flatbed trucks. The families came out carrying the photos, looking sad and crying. The cars drove away slowly. It was a very solemn and touching moment but also truly Cuban, since one of the trucks stalled and had to be pushed to start. A militante by my side groaned: "Oh, no, not now." The solemn procession started up, with the cars up front, the militia, families, guests of honor, and then the hundreds and hundreds of people.

The procession went to a newly built cemetery especially for the internacionalistas. The militia shot an honorary gun salute, and the brass band played the national anthem: "Que morir por la patria es vivir" (To die for the homeland is to live). Many people cried. The caskets and boxes were brought into the cemetery, which is on a hill. The guests of honor, the families, and the leaders from the municipality entered, while the rest of the people waited at the foot of the hill, outside. The first secretary of the Party made a short speech praising the young men. He said that they have given their lives for something important, which was especially clear now that Angola and Namibia were free. His voice broke during the speech, and many of the people watching cried as well. Finally he pronounced "Eternal Glory" to their memory, and the funeral was over.

That the funerals were meant to be and indeed became a ritual of national unity was clear to anyone who took part in them. It was an intensely emotional day, most of all for the families of the deceased and for internacionalistas who returned alive from their missions, but also for Cubans in general. Many in Palmera said that they cried when they saw the caskets and boxes being carried up to the cemetery.

The television news anchors who reported on the various funeral events throughout Cuba were dressed in uniform, and national and local newspapers printed their usually red-colored logos in black.

The funerals can also be seen as a rite of passage in which the young *combatientes* (fighters) came to symbolize one of the most important values of the revolution—sacrifice. The first part of the ceremony emphasized the private side of the young revolutionaries. At the wake, their families' grief was recognized and highlighted. The photos of the deceased showed them as private persons. The connection to the revolution was only indirect, in that militantes as well as medical staff cared for the families. Gradually, the emphasis shifted to the official aspect of the day. The honor guard gradually expanded to include important representatives of the revolution, culminating with the four highest officials of the municipality. When the caskets and boxes were carried to the cars to be driven to the cemetery, the photos were given to the families, but the Cuban flag remained reinforcing that the event had national importance.

The slow procession to the cemetery reminded everyone that these were young men who were dead and about to be buried. At the cemetery, they were placed in white marble slots in a special area created for them. By the time the first secretary proclaimed Eternal Glory to their memories, they had been transformed into heroes of the revolution.

The funerals included many symbolic aspects associated with the revolution, including the Cuban flags wrapped around the caskets and boxes and the playing of the national anthem. All the prominent guests were dressed in olive-green uniforms, the color of the FAR.[12] The honor guard was composed of young militia men and women, and the whole act had a solemn military touch to it that is far less common in other Cuban ceremonies.

At every important occasion, doctors and nurses are present to take care of people, but here the medical care became a symbol of the care the state had shown the families of the dead even before the ceremony. The attention was official; the doctors and nurses stayed with the families in the small house where they sat with their dead. The medical staff, dressed in white, took blood pressures and conversed with the family members to calm them down. But the families did not receive only physical attention. That their ideological and spiritual state was equally important was underlined by the fact that a Party member was present throughout the ceremony to help and support the families, thus implicitly pointing out that physical life is nothing if it is not accompanied by its ideological elements.

The ceremony also had national significance. The entire country was involved, which was evident in the mass media coverage and that the event was talked about among people everywhere, many of whom knew someone who had died. All of this contributed to the feeling of national unity and togetherness.

Feelings were at a high pitch that night when Fidel Castro made a speech, broadcast on television, at the central ceremony in Havana, accompanied by the president of Angola, José Eduardo Dos Santos. The speech was aggressive in tone toward the United States but also concerning the recent events in Eastern Europe. The militantes with whom I was watching were thrilled. Television sets were on all over the barrio, and after the speech it was clear that more people than usual had watched it. Once again Fidel asserted that Cuba would never stray from the road of socialism and that the despicable events in Eastern Europe, most certainly inspired by the CIA, would not be repeated in Cuba.

With almost theatrical irony, this day of national catharsis ended with an incident at the American base in Guantánamo in which U.S.

[12]The color is symbolically very important, and a magazine published by the FAR is called *Verde Olivo*.

soldiers shot at Cuban soldiers. The newspapers reported the next day that people spontaneously took to the streets to protest.

By this time, Cuban leaders most certainly knew, and the people suspected, that the economic situation in Cuba would quickly deteriorate. With the loss of the Eastern European countries as trade partners and the Soviet Union leaning more and more toward the West, it had become increasingly evident that Cuba would face serious problems. Whether intentionally or not, the funeral events provided a perfect opportunity to reinforce relations between the Party, its leaders, and the people.

Political ceremonies can easily become "empty" in Cuba because they occur so often, but this ritual had all the elements necessary for success as strong personal emotions blended with feelings of national pride and achievement. 2,289 persons had been killed during Cuba's missions abroad (*Granma*, 8, Dec. 1989). Those who unfortunately met this fate had now received recognition. The revolutionary act—the sacrifice for and fulfillment of the task of perfecting the revolution—had once again been defined as the basis for the revolution.

[7]

Conclusions

By describing different aspects of life in Palmera, I have tried to provide a multifaceted picture of what the people themselves call *the revolution*. The hegemonic political ideology, the centralist political structure, and the planned economy pervade everyday life. These ideas and structures, which to a great extent are modeled after those in the Soviet Union, are new to Cuban society. But traditional ideas also remain an essential part of Cuban life (cf. Hann 1993; Lancaster 1988, 1992; Lane 1981; Potter and Potter 1990). Being generous is just as important today as it always has been, although acts of generosity have to occur in the context of the rationed economy. Reciprocity continues and is sometimes reinforced within the planned economy, where information about where to find goods becomes a main commodity used to reinforce social relations but where gifts, loans, and exchanges also are important economic transactions. The gender system, although it has changed a lot structurally, still includes attitudes that reinforce the differences between and the separation of women and men.

Ideology in Everyday Life

No one in Cuba can avoid being affected by socialist ideology in one way or another, whether one accepts its premises or not. As I have mentioned, socialism in Cuba is a hegemonic ideology, (Gramsci 1971) meaning, as Antonio Gramsci said, it is the "rule" (Williams

1977:108), that is, socialist political structures and organizations dominate the whole society—thereby making it difficult to realize alternatives. Those who want to start a political party or a political organization are breaking the law, and up to 1994 those who wanted to find new ways of supporting themselves could not do so partly because it was not allowed, but also because of difficulties in securing materials and the means of distribution, which were in the hands of the state. The ideology is also hegemonic in that all political ideas emanate from only one political party, and other political ideas must therefore be expressed clandestinely or not at all. The "folk versions" of ideology modify this normative and ideological domination. Here I agree with James C. Scott (1985), who said that even a dominant ideology is subject to "negotiations" whereby those who formulate the ideology must accept divergencies and even incorporate them into the dominant ideology.[1] In Palmera this is evident in the system of reciprocity and the gender system. But first and foremost the acceptance and view of an ideology depend on the experiences and the practices of those who are affected by it. When the people in Palmera feel that their experiences are not compatible with the ideological messages they are hearing, they evaluate them and when necessary reject them, although they might not always be able to express how they feel. Likewise, they accept and promote those ideological messages that are strengthened by their own experiences.

The official ideology, however, has many aspects and reaches very far into people's lives. There is no doubt that it is about *power*—who should have it and what legitimizes it, but also the structures that organize it.[2] In Palmera the power structure is evident in everyday life in the hierarchy of all administrative and political institutions, and whether people deal with the Party, FMC, CDR, or Poder Popular, they are reminded of their centralized structures. People turn to their leaders for practical help in personal and community matters. In this face-to-face society, many people know their leaders, and the leaders usually have a casual and open relationship with the people,

[1]Gramsci (1971:161) has also pointed this out, although he was talking about economism.

[2]This discussion builds on Thompson 1986.

although as we have seen, in some remote villages the people may never have seen their leaders.

The hierarchy of the community is also visible in ceremonies and rituals, in which the leaders are symbolically separated from the people by their physical placement on a stage or podium. This emphasizes the role of leader but also the uniqueness of the leaders as persons. Further, leaders who are invited to ceremonies or meetings often do not have direct connections to the event but are present to enhance its importance.

Power can be used in many different ways. Cuba's leaders have certainly used their power to improve the lives of ordinary people. But what people had to sacrifice for these improvements was a certain amount of freedom. Some people appreciate the material improvements and the opportunity to take part in the mass organizations and in the Poder Popular. To them, it does not matter that they cannot vote for more than one party, or read newspapers other than those that the Party controls. They remember that what they had before was neither freedom nor democracy. Others compare Cuba now with what it could be and are disgusted by the fact that they are not allowed to criticize the Party and the system, that they cannot open their own businesses, that they cannot vote for whatever party they want, and that they cannot leave the country when they want.

Power is also present in Cuban society in the form of "collective memories" (Connerton 1989) of repression and in the tacit knowledge that power can be exercised erratically and incomprehensibly. For ordinary people, the centralized political structure is difficult to control. Cubans discovered this already in 1961, when their leaders declared the revolution to be socialist. Many of those who had supported and even fought with the rebels hardly knew what socialism meant, even less about being socialists. Some chose to leave the country when they decided that the revolution was taking a turn they did not like; others stayed on and accepted the new ideology; still others were already convinced of the good of socialism.

To implement and disseminate an ideology, especially a hegemonic ideology, also involves *social control*, which may be exerted through an emphasis on normative behavior or by means of repression. A foreigner coming to Cuba who has heard about the repression of communist systems often finds Cuba a very free and easy place to be. Foreigners can travel anywhere and talk to anyone they like. Cubans themselves are restricted in many ways, however. Militantes are not supposed to become too close to foreigners, and political representatives are supposed to keep an eye on those in their neighborhoods who deviate in one way or another, and when they consider that someone has done something wrong, the system closes down on that person. A person who shows too much interest in going abroad can lose his or her job, and someone who tries to emigrate is often left in limbo for a long time, without a job or a place in society, while his or her application is being processed.

This invisible power is perhaps the most difficult and frightening to live with. Cubans are very skillful at balancing their desire to criticize the political system with the need to remain silent. In the case of the asamblea, we saw that delegates could deliver rather harsh criticism while always keeping within the limits of the acceptable political line. It is difficult for an outsider to judge where these limits lie. The Party and Fidel Castro are never criticized directly, but the Party is constantly criticized indirectly in complaints about the ineffectiveness and malfunctioning of the society. Since open protests are banned, protests take the form of covert and hidden expression, such as showing disinterest or not participating in events or meetings. At least in Palmera, the question of *who* is doing the criticizing is crucial. A well-known and trusted militante can express thoughts for which a person who is "marginal" to the system might be sanctioned. Further, the sanctions, like the protests, often are diffuse, such as not being promoted or losing a position without ever being told why. This leads to an insecurity that may be the most effective repressive aspect of the system. It is based in knowledge about people who were handled capriciously by official institutions and in knowledge that the possibility of sanctions exists. As in all political systems, the person who lives a quiet life within the limits of the system has nothing to fear. Conformity guarantees freedom, which is the essence of effective social control.

Ideology is also about *visions*, about what we want to do with our lives and our society. The vision in Cuba, as in all societies, naturally has as its starting point the old society. It is said that no one should have to go to bed hungry or be banned from a cinema, a restaurant, or a job because of her or his color. Women should not be discriminated against in work and should be independent. No one should have the right to exploit another human being. Equal opportunities should exist for everyone. No one should have to quit school because his or her parents do not have the money to pay the fees. Everyone should be able to live with dignity. But visions often collide with reality. Old attitudes die hard, and although female and black Cubans have the same rights as everyone else, prejudices still exist against them. To obtain dollars for the country, the leaders who advocated equal opportunities now must allow a double economy to exist composed of the "Cuban Sector" and the "tourist sector." Because of international economic and political decisions, the leaders who wanted no one to go to bed hungry now have to guide the country through a special period when food is almost as scarce as other goods.

The vision of the socialist revolution also contains a moral component (cf. Valdés 1992), the wish to create "a new person." This is realized in the almost puritanical focus on the need to work hard and to sacrifice. The idea of the revolutionary *act* has been at the core of the revolution ever since Che Guevara introduced the idea of voluntary work. With that the revolutionary act changed from an act involving soldiers in a revolutionary army to the business of everyone, including women. Women still have total responsibility for child care and housework, however, and can seldom take part in the most prestigious revolutionary tasks.

Ideology is also about *social cementing*, about creating and strengthening feelings of unity. The basis of this unity in Cuba is patriotism. In the love of their country, people with many different views can unite. Many men and women in Palmera are passionate patriots. Mostly this is formulated as a love for Cuba as a country, as their home, a place where people are cheerful, fun-loving, and relaxed. Depending on one's political views, this may or may not include the socialist system or the revolution. Those who are loyal to the system believe that Cuba is a good place to live *because* of socialism. Others feel that it is a good place to live *in spite of* the system.

Cubans' pride in their society is strengthened through ceremonies and rituals that highlight and commemorate historical events and heroes of the revolution (cf. Connerton 1989). History is very much on the minds of Cubans, perhaps especially those in Palmera and the Oriente, where so many important events took place not only during the revolutionary war but also earlier in Cuban history. From primary school on, children are taught to be proud of their heroes and their history. Recurring ceremonies like the big rally on 26 July, the enactment of the Moncada attack, and the commeoration of Che and Camilo, when flowers are thrown in the sea, remind people of both their Cuban and their revolutionary identities (see Rosendahl 1992a and 1992b). The burial of the internacionalistas was an exceptional but extremely powerful demonstration of unity.

Social cementing is also accomplished by comparing Cuba to other countries and by emphasizing the threat from the United States. This threat leads most Cubans to say that they would defend their country to the last drop of their blood. Social cementing is also done in rhetoric in which the improved material and social conditions, the classlessness and equal opportunities in Cuba, and the fact that everyone has to pull together to fulfill the goals of the revolution are emphasized. Examples from history are used by leaders and followers alike to reinforce the improvements that have occurred in many people's lives.

The rhetoric describing Cuba as the best of all worlds is often crude and exaggerated, which at times creates a backlash of bitterness and criticism of the system, a refusal to see anything good in it. The patriotism overrides most of the criticism, however, and even the most ardent critics defend Cuba when they feel it is under attack from outside.

It might be an exaggeration to call the Cuban political ideology a political religion (see Lane 1981), but its socialist ideology certainly has religious overtones (cf. Valdés 1992).[3] The "sacralization of the existing political order" (Lane 1981:42) makes it self-perpetuating and difficult to question. There is a mytho-logic as Edmund Leach (1976) calls it, a logic that functions only within its own system. This includes the extremely rational view of the world that Cuban socialism presents. Not only practical problems but people's attitudes are treated as if they can be changed rationally with just enough will

[3]For an interesting discussion of nationalism and its relation to religion, see Kapferer 1988.

power and work. When this is proven wrong, time and time again, mistakes are interpreted as tests of the system that should lead to ways to better it, not as failures in the system itself (see Rosendahl 1992a). Many problems in the system are also interpreted as being caused by evils external to it. The socialist ideology provides primarily a "model for" (Geertz 1973:93–94) society and to a large extent disregards any "model of" society, since that is more incompatible with the ideal (cf. Lane 1981: 25). Cuba's political ideology explains what this ideal society would be and declares the goal of the revolution to be this ideal society—a communist society where each person should receive from society in accordance with his or her needs, but also contribute to society in accordance with his or her capabilities. The evolutionist element in Marxism makes it possible to see socialism as a step on the road to communism.

The political ideology in Cuba also resembles a religion in that it "claims authority not only over the political affairs of a society but over all of society" (Lane 1981:42). This is very clear in Cuban socialism, which, like its Chinese counterpart but in contrast to the Soviet variety (Lane 1981; Potter and Potter 1990), is normative at the individual level. Individuals are expected to pursue the ideals of sacrifice, selflessness, and loyalty, which are also Christian ideals. The representatives of the system ideally should be flawless (cf. Potter and Potter 1990) since they are the connection between the "sacred," in this case the "good, ideal society," and the mundane, the practical everyday policies (cf. Leach 1976). As we have seen, the ideology "offers explanations which not only help individuals to comprehend but also induce them to accept and endure life's sufferings for the sake of some greater good" (Lane 1981:41). This is clear when Cuban leaders ask people to sacrifice, also a concept with religious overtones, for the revolution. It is even more evident, of course, in the ultimate sacrifice, in which the revolutionary gives his or her life for the greater good.

Also like a religion, there is both the "pure" ideology, the official ideology presented in texts and by the leaders, and the popular or folk versions, which are a mixture of the ideas, norms, and traditions shared by individuals at all levels. In these folk versions, socialism of the theoretical, Marxist-Leninist kind is not especially salient. Many people have very little knowledge of what pure socialism is. Their attitudes toward the system and its leaders are based on the political realities of thirty-five years and on their general view of what constitutes a just society, which may or may not be socialist.

Opinions about the Party and Socialism

In Cuba as in other countries, people hold many different opinions about the government. And, as elsewhere, these opinions depend on people's positions in society and on their experiences (cf. Hannerz, Liljeström, and Löfgren, eds. 1982; Rosendahl 1985).

The biggest divide in attitudes toward socialism and the revolution is that between militantes and non-Party members. Militantes, both male and female, defend the system vehemently. They interpret difficulties and problems as caused by outside forces (mainly the U.S. embargo) or as steps in a not yet completed historical process. When people are accepted into the Party, they pledge to defend socialism. Militantes thus defend ideas disseminated by the Party either because they feel they must or because they truly believe in them. Some militantes are critical of certain ideas but would never advocate their own opinion before testing it on the members of their base group.

Among non-Party members, a whole spectrum of opinions is represented. Some are as loyal to the Party and socialism as the militantes but have either not been accepted into the Party or have refused membership.[4] They take part in the mobilizations and the mass organizations out of a real interest and a wish to contribute to society. In this category are some of the leaders of the municipality, representatives in the mass organizations, and delegates to the Poder Popular.

Most non-Party members, however, are rather uninterested in politics. They do not oppose the system and vote in the elections to the

[4]In the late 1980s membership in the Party was restricted for professionals and white-collar workers since the leadership felt that the proportion of manual workers was too small. Those who are suspected of or known to be homosexuals are not accepted. Those who told me that they refused membership in the Party referred to their heavy workloads and said that if they were to become members, they would want to give the Party their full attention and effort.

Poder Popular, but they take part in mobilizations and mass organizations reluctantly. To them, the socialist ideology is ever-present in everyday life, as a backdrop to other activities and events.

Still others would like to see a complete change in the system. They try to avoid taking part in Party activities and criticize the system as much as they can.

Cubans' views of socialism and the revolution are very much influenced by their experiences before the revolution. Not surprisingly, these views seem to follow former class lines. Those who were very poor and led hard lives before the revolution are much more likely to be in favor of the politics of today. They can endure much without losing faith in the revolution and the Party because the conditions in which they lived antes were worse. They also seem to convey these feelings to their children, who more often than not have the same attitude. Those who suffered a material loss (expropriation of land or other property) as a result of the revolution do not have as much indulgence with the shortcomings.

A person's place in society today also affects his or her view of socialism and the revolution, although less starkly than former class positions. Private farmers seem to be less engaged in the politics of the country and very often keep to themselves, in spite of efforts by the ANAP and the Party to incorporate them into cooperatives.[5] Those who have high-status positions are either directly involved in the political structure (the Party and the Poder Popular), and therefore publicly demonstrate their loyalty to socialism, or work in positions (doctors, teachers) that are intimately tied to political performance (see Rosendahl 1992a).

For those with low-status jobs, the situation is more complicated. Many come from poor families and therefore are pleased with the improvement in conditions in Cuban society. Some become militantes, thereby elevating their status and effecting a strong link to the revolution. There is also ideologically based upgrading of the most

[5]The ANAP is the mass organization for peasants. It tries to incorporate as many peasants as possible into the various cooperatives in Cuba. One type of cooperative is the CPA, in which the members work together on state-owned land and share in the profits of the cooperative. Another is the CCS, an organization for private peasants who have joined together so they can get loans and credits from the state. The most recent type is the UBPC, created on former state farms.

humble jobs, so that, for example, productive agricultural and construction workers are made to feel they are making essential contributions to society. They are featured as "celebrities" in ceremonies and in articles and photographs in the newspaper, thereby linking them to the revolution.

Color also affects people's views of the revolution. Those who experienced racism antes often feel loyalty to the revolution, if only because they and their children are better treated today.

Some people in low-status occupations are very critical of the revolution. They are disappointed and feel that they have not gained as much as they should from the change. In Palmera this is not very common, but in Havana many young men from the Old Town who come from poor families show their contempt for socialism by working the black market and generally living on the margins of society. In Palmera differences in status are not very pronounced, but in the bigger cities there are cultural and intellectual elites whose lives are very different from those of the workers. Whereas political leaders at the municipal level have few privileges, those at the national level live rather privileged and secluded lives.

No direct link can be seen between education, age, and attitude toward the revolution. A large part of the Cuban population has grown up during the revolution. They attended schools that taught the ideology of the revolution, and they grew up taking part in the Pioneers or in the UJC, the youth organization. Some are critical of the government and demand better opportunities, more goods, and more freedom. Many others, however, are as loyal to the revolution as are older Cubans. Here again their positions in society, and family experiences antes are important. Quite a few Cuban academics are very critical of socialism. There is also much stronger self-censorship than among farmers or workers, however, so that it is difficult to know what their actual attitudes are.

There seem to be very few differences between men and women in their attitudes toward socialism and the revolution. This is perhaps surprising considering how different their lives are. Most women are now incorporated into society through work or politics, and their position overall has improved during the revolution. Older women might feel that they are lucky to have more freedom and more opportunities today, but most women also have the double workload of job and home. This leads to criticism and weariness with all the demands from the leaders. Nonetheless, in general, I did not find the women to be more critical than the men. Some women are frustrated because they feel that the society has not changed very much with respect to gender roles and machismo. Both women and men, still accept the gendered structure of society, however, and most women look at machismo as something they should expect if also sometimes frustrating.

Features That Have Sustained the Revolution

There are four features of the Cuban revolution that have strengthened it and enabled it to continue for more than three decades. First, until 1990 many Cubans clearly had an improved standard of living. Memories of the grim situation before the revolution are important here, too. Second, the personal experience of participating in the revolution, which people in Palmera gained through fighting, helping, and sympathizing with the rebels, is certainly important. Those who did not participate directly have benefited from the collective local memory, which the leaders constantly reinforce. Third, Cubans hear a strong, constant, and homogeneous ideological message about the benefits of the revolution. This would mean very little, however, if people could not in some way recognize their experiences in these messages. Fourth, and finally, in Cuba traditional male gender ideals are very similar to ideals for the revolutionary.

The improvement in the standard of living was a very conscious undertaking that occurred in part because of aid and trade with the Soviet Union and in part because of the moral emphasis on voluntary work and socialist competition, which have improved the otherwise flawed system of Cuban production. Important also is the relatively equal distribution of scarce resources. This has affected and molded people's attitudes, and although they complain about the lack of goods and choices, most people in Cuba approve of the fairly equal system of sharing.

Participation is one of the most important ideas in Cuban socialism. Having participated in the revolutionary war is important, but so is taking part in voluntary work, in the Party, and in the representative organs of the state today in making Cubans feel they are part of the ongoing revolution.

Leaders very consciously use ideological messages to reinforce people's sense of personal loyalty and connection to the revolution. By using the same messages, and sometimes almost the same words, vertically at all levels of society (in the municipality, in the province, and in the nation), horizontally (in schools, the mass media, and organizations), and in different forums (rituals, ceremonies, speeches, and government acts), ideological messages have enormous impact. Rituals, ceremonies, and speeches have such an emotional charge for many Cubans because the ideological message is rooted in their personal experiences. As discussed in chapter 5, for many people, their own experiences of hardship before the revolution, of participating in building the revolution, and of living lives that they feel are just validate the ideological messages communicated by their leaders.

The last important feature that has sustained socialism in Cuba is that the traditional ideal for men as "private individuals" has been transferred to the political arena and become the ideal for leaders and "good revolutionaries," most of whom are men. The male gender ideal fits well with socialist ideals of strength, audacity, responsibility, initiative, and courage, and in many circumstances, being a good revolutionary is the same as being a good man. These ideals are embraced by both men and women, and for this reason Cubans can accept an active yet sometimes paternalistic style of leadership. These ideals reinforce the role of the male charismatic leader and help explain why so few women had leading positions in the revolutionary war and after and why very few women are leaders today.

Epilogue

Anthropologists often present their material in ways that sacrifice the image of continuous social processes on the altar of textual clarity. I have probably also fallen into this trap, because up to 1991, when I completed my fieldwork in Palmera, the changes in Cuba were gradual and partial. Today, however, the social changes are rapid and radical. These events have been analyzed in books and articles, often in the implicit or explicit hope of predicting the result of these processes. For me this is not an important aim, but I do want to discuss how these changes might affect some of my analyses and conclusions.

The Special Period

In the winter of 1990, after the período especial had begun, a friend in Palmera who was very much involved in the politics of the municipality said to me that he feared that the economic situation in Cuba would deteriorate for years before it improved again. He referred to the concept of *opción zero*, which Fidel Castro and other national leaders used when talking about a warlike situation in which each region would have to become self-supporting. He was proved right. This period has now lasted for seven years. Until now this special period could be divided into two stages. From 1990 to 1994, the economic situation deteriorated steadily as Cuba lost its support from and trade with the former Soviet Union and the former socialist states in Eastern Europe. At the end of 1994, the situation improved somewhat as new international economic relations and internal economic measures were developed and joint ventures begun that helped stabilize the economy. From the beginning of the special period, the political leaders told the people of the drastic changes that were necessary and warned them that worse times would come. In Palmera, as in the rest of Cuba, people were used to scarcity and difficulties, however, and they probably never imagined that the situation would become so critical.

When I returned to Cuba in the summer of 1993, the situation was grave. Large cuts had been made in food rations, and gasoline, electricity, and other goods and services were in short supply. Food was scarce. People were not starving, but they could definitely not eat as much as they had before and they complained that there was no lard or cooking oil and that the food therefore had no taste. A disease was spreading that affected the eyes and legs of many people and that was later diagnosed as caused by the drastic drop in food intake (Rosling 1994). There was no kerosene for the stoves, and the women had to cook with wood or coal. Transportation had broken down, since there were no spare parts and no gasoline. Bicycles from China were now the principal means of transportation. In Havana all the streets and even the highway from the airport to the center were filled with people pedaling to and from work. Car parks were turned into parking lots for bicycles. People's skill at bicycling was not very great, and accidents were frequent, some even leading to death.

The use of electricity was severely restricted. There were *apagones* (cuts in electricity) that lasted for hours which led some to joke: "Here we do not have apagones, we have *lumbrones* (a longer period of light)." These outages made life very difficult. There was no water for hours on end in buildings that depended on electric pumps. After dark, no housework could be done, no books or papers read, no television watched, and no meetings held. People often just stood or sat around in their yards smoking and chatting with their neighbors.

People were out of work because factories and other workplaces had closed down. In Havana adult men sat on sidewalks in the middle of the day, a very unusual sight before. They still received 70 percent of their salary, but the nonactivity was difficult. Many people were sent or volunteered to go out to the countryside to work in agriculture, which was now the most important part of the Cuban economy. The lack of transportation made it almost impossible for many to come to work on time, and the difficulty in finding food made it necessary for people to stay home from work to stand in line when a chicken or some fish arrived at the shop.

After the food rations were reduced and the free markets were closed, the black market grew explosively and most food was now bought through the black market. Those who had to buy on the black market found that their salary sufficed for less and less. In the summer of 1993, there were two black markets, one with payment in dollars and the other in pesos. The really attractive goods could be found in the dollar market. The prices in both markets were exorbitant—250 pesos for a pair of shoes, 1,500 pesos for a pair of jeans, 300 pesos for a large bottle of shampoo, 60 pesos for a bar of soap, 20 pesos for a pound of rice, and 60 pesos for a chicken. Salaries were at the same level as before, however—on average, 120 to 170 pesos per month.

Crime soared, and stories about terrible, violent crimes circulated. I think these stories more reflected people's insecurity than reality, although organized stealing had become more frequent. Since all goods were collected and redistributed at a state market, the goods in the black market had to be stolen from the state warehouses in one way or another. This meant that state supplies became even scarcer. Some farmers also saw the opportunity to make money by selling their surpluses directly to customers, sometimes for dollars, instead of sending them to the state stock. The desire for dollars was high, and the rate on the black market in July 1993 was one dollar for sixty pesos.[1]

In the summer of 1994, the grim situation led to the first open demonstrations on the streets of Havana in many years and an exodus of people left the country in *balsas* (homemade rafts) headed for the United States. So many arrived in Florida that the U.S. government started to send the refugees back to the U.S. base in Guantánamo. This and an agreement that Cuba made with the United States to

[1]By 1994, the rate had gone up to 140 pesos.

try to stop the illegal emigrants in return for more legal migration temporarily stopped the balseros.

Economic Reforms

In an effort to save the country and relieve the Cubans' burdens, the government introduced several economic measures and reforms. In 1993, Fidel Castro announced in his annual 26 July speech that Cubans could now legally possess dollars. Depenalization had been long awaited, and the first thing I had been told when I returned to Cuba was that there was a rumor that Fidel would announce this change. For some this was welcome news, while others worried about the consequences. Those who had or could get hold of dollars at this point were people with relatives abroad, those who worked in the tourist trade, and black marketeers who had changed dollars illegally on the street. The people who did not and would not have access to the dollar market were those who were the most loyal to the system and who had sacrificed a lot for the revolution and lived within the limits and laws of the country. They worried about the consequences of the "free" dollar and feared they would end up in the bottom half of an emerging class-based society.[2]

The winners in the new system were the new entrepreneurs (private farmers and the self-employed) and those working in the tourist sector. About one hundred occupations in services were opened to self-employment. Street markets were opened, and, especially in Havana, vendors began to sell all kinds of artifacts, trinkets, shoes, snacks, and drinks in stalls on the streets. A new kind of cooperative (UBPC) was introduced on former state farms. The people who were working there were given the right to cultivate the land and to sell the crops and use the surplus for investment and profit sharing. They were also given plots for their own use. Markets were allowed in which farmers could sell their produce at market prices. And to earn money for the state treasury, taxes were introduced on some incomes and profits.

[2]For a closer examination of the effect of the special period on the self-image of the people in Palmera, see Rosendahl (1997).

The most significant change was also one of the first measures to be introduced, namely, joint ventures with other countries. Join ventures had been initiated in tourism in the 1980s, but the number increased significantly during the early years of the 1990s, when areas such as mining, oil, and telecommunications became involved. In this way "capitalism" entered Cuba through the "back door."

Tourism is the sector that has expanded the most in recent years and is expected to bring in dollars quickly to the country. Large hotels have been built all over the country that provide mass and luxury accommodations for tourists from Europe, Canada, and Latin America. Before the special period, the tourist sector was already a sore spot for many Cubans who felt the injustice in not being allowed to buy the luxury items available to tourists or to enjoy their "extravagant" life style. During the special period these differences became even more obvious. While Cubans had to walk or bicycle to work because of the lack of fuel, tourist taxis swooped down the streets of Havana, and while Cuban families did not have more than vegetable soup to eat, tourists ate abundantly in dollar restaurants. While Cubans had to stand in line for hours to enter a restaurant, tourists walked right in, and while Cuban children had to walk around in tattered shoes, the dollar shops sold shoes of all shapes, forms, and colors. This gave rise to great resentment among many Cubans. When Cubans could use dollars, the division was no longer between tourists and Cubans, but between Cubans *with* dollars and those *without*.

The increase in tourism also opened up old wounds. Prostitution, which had been almost nonexistent some years earlier, suddenly increased. Young girls sold their bodies for a meal or a pair of shoes. The *jinteteras* and *jineteros* as they are called offer all kinds of services or goods to the tourists in exchange for dollars, a marriage proposal, or an invitation to another country.

The economic measures brought relief to many households, especially in Havana and other larger cities. Although the prices were high at the farmers' markets, meat, viandas, and vegetables were available. The release of the dollar to Cubans made the rates of exchange on the black market drop so that in May 1996 it was down to twenty pesos per dollar. The tourist sector became an attractive job area because of the chances of meeting foreigners and of receiving tips in dollars, which made the workers in the tourist sector privileged. Those Cubans who could pay in dollars also could enjoy the luxuries of the tourist sector.[3]

The Special Period in Palmera

Palmera was affected by the economic crisis, of course, although less so than Havana. Still, there were fewer cars, buses, and trucks on the streets of Limones when I returned to Palmera in the summer of 1993 and more bicycles, horse carts, and mules. People walked or cycled, often with heavy loads, and those who were lucky enough to have a horse or a mule rode to work and leisure activities. The parallel markets were closed, and the shelves in the shops gaped even more empty than before.

People still sauntered down the main street in Limones, stopping to chat and flirt with friends and acquaintances, but the atmosphere was different. When I asked people by way of greeting how they were, they listlessly said "Ya tu sabes" (Well, you know) or "Regular" (So, so). Women who had been plump and voluptuous were thin, and men who had carried their big stomachs with pride were now very thin.

In Palmera food is a symbol of the good life. This became even more clear with the lack of it. Eating two meals, preferably of viandas, rice and beans, and meat or fish, freshly cooked in lard, was seen not only as a physical but a "cultural" necessity; it was part of being a real Cuban. Food is also connected with the ideal of generosity, which is equally important to being a real Cuban. It was difficult to be generous when there was nothing to offer, when friends and acquaintances could not be invited to sit down and eat at dinnertime or when parties could not be given. If the people of Palmera had been preoccupied with getting hold of food and other items before, they were now obsessed with it. People activated all their relationships to buy, exchange, or barter food or other items. The inventiveness never ceased. Closely linked to this obsession was

[3]For other accounts of the special period and of Cuba's new economy, see Bengelsdorf 1994; Cardoso and Helwege 1992; Eckstein 1994; IRELA 1994.

their notion of the body. A well-nourished and voluptuous body had been looked upon as a manifestation of the good in life, of a secure standard of living, of a dignified life, and of lustful eroticism. When people suddenly lost weight, the body became a manifestation of the difficulties in society. It became obvious that the good life was crumbling. It was difficult to display a sexy figure when one's clothes hung loosely on one's body.

The food situation was better in Palmera than in the larger cities since people could buy and receive food from their friends and relatives who had farms in the country. The standard of living, however, which had been rather high in Palmera, had radically fallen in only two years. Some of my former neighbors grew plantains, yucca, and other tubers near their buildings, and some kept small piglets on their balconies. Other friends tried to keep pigs and goats in their back yards, but they were often stolen.

Criminality had also increased in Palmera. There had been very few crimes before, but now people had to guard their animals and keep their bicycles indoors to avoid theft. Juana had her newly washed clothes stolen from her balcony, and Abel, who lived in a small house in Limones where no one was home during the day, lost his hens from the back yard. A tourist had been murdered in Palmera, and there were rumors about violent robberies. There was a feeling of insecurity in the air, which manifested itself in suspicion of outsiders and even of neighbors and acquaintances.

The black market in Palmera had also become a more common source of nonluxury goods than before. A friend explained how people spread the risks of working the black market by distributing their goods in various directions. A person who got hold of a lot of garlic, for instance, split it up among a few distributors who in turn sold their lots to subdistributors, and so on. The price naturally increased at every level.

When I returned in the summer of 1993, I also noticed a change in the opinions of my friends in Palmera. It was not a total reversal but a slight shift in their discourse about society. Those who had been loyal believers in socialism and the revolution were still loyal and expressed the belief that the difficulties would pass, but there was also a hint of resignation and sometimes also of shame in their comments. Ana, who had always been a vanguard worker and a loyal revolutionary, said: "I have stopped worrying about food and other things. If I get it, I get it; otherwise, I will have to solve the problem when it arises. There is no use in worrying all the time." Maria, also an ardent revolutionary, refused to let me take a picture of her cooking on her coal stove in her garden because she felt shame, she said, that Cuba had become so "backward." Those who had accepted the socialist ideas and felt that they shared in the construction of the new society experienced great personal distress because Cuba's social project seemed to have gone astray. In Palmera quite a lot of people expressed the same feelings Maria did.

In May 1995, when I once again spent a week in Palmera, the atmosphere was a bit more optimistic. The economic situation was still difficult, however, especially obtaining imported goods such as soap, shampoo, detergent, and shoes and clothes. One of my best friends in Limones, a vanguard worker who was loyal to the revolution and always participating in voluntary work and other activities, wrote to me in March 1995: "Mona, all I say is complaining, but we are in a clothing crisis in the house. *Me da pena* (I'm ashamed) to tell you, but that is the fact . . . It does not matter if they are used clothes, but if you could collect some from your friends it would not be bad." I can see this proud woman squirming because she had to beg me for *anything*, let alone clothes. When I lived in Limones, she and her family often fed me and helped me with everything.

People in Palmera, as someone said, had resigned themselves to the new situation. In my opinion, it was more that they had adapted, since the idea of *inventar* (invent solutions) had reached unbelievable levels. Almost everyone in Limones cultivated tubers and vegetables and kept animals—pigs, sheep, and goats. Families made their own detergent from tree sprigs, crocheted shoes, and remodeled old clothes into new designs. People were still slim but had regained some weight, and many had adjusted to their new figures and rather liked them. Along the beautiful coast of Palmera, three new hotels had been erected, one of which was an enormous construction meant to cater to charter tourism from Canada and other countries. Quite a few people from the municipality had gotten jobs in the new hotels along the coast, which brought dollars in the form of tips to some families.[4] A *chopping* (dollar shop) had opened in Limones where attractive goods could be bought. A new work ethic had also become evident so that in discussions "ordinary" people claimed that they had been bad workers and had to take more responsibility and work harder. This was what the leaders and some militantes had always said, but now this idea was also presented in daily discourse by those who never would have mentioned it before. This new morality is probably partly rooted in the work rules and ethics that capitalist joint-ventures firms in the tourism industry have introduced. I was told that people have been fired from the hotels for not coming to work on time and for stealing from the workplace. These ideas have probably also taken hold because people have seen that when they worked hard at cultivating and tending their animals, their efforts resulted in benefits for their families.

The new economy has not brought only benefits to Palmera, however. Social differences are now clearer than before, and those who work in tourism are the winners. Professionals, such as teachers and administrators, are the losers since except for those who have relatives abroad, they have no legal way to earn dollars. A new joke is that "now the only way of surviving is to have *fé* (faith)," which today means *familiares en el extranjero* (relatives abroad).

For those who have no dollars, the economic situation is the reverse of what it was in the late 1980s. Then most people had too much money since there was little to buy. Today, since salaries are the same as before the special period or have increased only marginally, most people do not have enough money even for necessities. The farmers' markets do not function well in Palmera. Few farmers sell their goods in Limones or in other towns since they get higher prices in the big city. Onions, garlic, and sometimes yucca or other viandas are sold, but there is hardly any meat and the prices are high.

The food rations on the libreta are now divided into two parts, half of it given at the beginning of the month and the other half in the middle of the month. Often items that ought to be on the libreta are not available. In May 1995, Palmera households received their

[4]The tips in the tourist hotels are pooled and shared equally by everyone at the end of the month, so that even workers who are not directly in contact with tourists receive the same amount as the others.

first bottle of cooking oil in five months. Meat is extremely scarce, and when it is available it is always ground. The most common source of animal protein is fish.

Social and Cultural Changes

Naturally, the profound economic changes have affected social and cultural aspects of life in Cuba. Much of what I have discussed in this book has been affected, although in different ways. As we have seen, the household economy, which is directly linked to the national economy, has been most affected. Changes in male-female attitudes and in the division of labor will take longer to occur. Some women who were interviewed as part of a Cuban study claimed that their husbands helped much more at home, because of the difficulties of getting food and other goods.[5] This was not evident in Palmera in 1995. The women were doing just as much in the house as before. The extended family, has become increasingly important, however. Retired grandmothers and grandfathers are invaluable to the family since they have time to stand in line, trying to obtain whatever there is on the market. By pooling their resources, families can sometimes buy some of the extremely expensive goods on the black market and in the farmers' markets. Maria, a young woman who was pregnant with her first child, told me that she received extra food rations on her family doctor's prescription and that members of her large extended family gave her the best of their food.

Given that revolutionary and male ideals are so closely linked, the economic situation should affect the leaders' power as well. One can only speculate, but it is probable that if the male leaders fail and can no longer be the mediators of a good life, they could meet with the same contempt that men with "horns" receive: they could be seen as weak and useless. A male leader who is seen as having lost his cojones or balls has definitely also lost his legitimacy as a leader.

The events of the special period have profoundly affected the

[5]Personal communication with Elena Díaz, Programa Flacso, Havana.

identity and self-image of many Cubans.[6] The new economy is leading to new strategies, new values, and a new social structure. Emerging social divisions follow in the wake of the economic divisions. It is obvious to people today that not every one has equal opportunities. Ownership of dollars is the clearest dividing line, but the opportunity to be self-employed is also critical. Private farmers who work hard cultivating crops and tending animals can make large profits by selling their products at the farmers' markets or to friends and acquaintances. Artisans and other self-employed workers can sell their products at a profit and also increase their standard of living. Those who work in the tourist sector or in joint-venture companies earn tips in dollars or other benefits that help solve immediate problems.[7] Those who do not have any of these advantages have to scrape by, watching the value of their money decrease and trying to get scarce resources to last as long as possible. For these families, their salaries are no longer sufficient to allow them to live the good life. Still, the basic assets everyone gets from the state are divided equally, so that all children can go to school, people can be treated gratis by doctors and nurses, and food can be bought inexpensively on the libereta. Further, personal inventiveness and initiative can lead to an improvement in the standard of living, and those with it have gained back some of the dignity that they felt they were losing.

Recently, many non-Cuban commentators, especially in newspapers, have speculated not only about *whether* Castro will fall but *when*. They have given simplistic explanations for the survival of the revolution, tying it only to the improved standard of living and the stark repression. These analysts have concluded that the political system of Cuba will fall immediately, since the standard of living has dropped and, they believe, the government is losing its grip on the citizens. The special period has shown, however, that although the improved standard of living has been an important factor in Cubans' support of the revolution, there is no simple connection between the

[6]For further discussions of this, see Rosendahl (1997).

[7]Cuba now has a convertible peso that is paid to workers in some sectors. it can only be used within Cuba, but has the same value as a U.S. dollar.

standard of living and loyalty to the revolution. What many of these commentators have overlooked is the role of the Cuban people. People in Palmera are thinking, reflecting, acting individuals. They might complain, and they might sometimes balance like tightrope walkers at the limits of accepted political expression, but most workers and farmers in Palmera do not just accept what their leaders tell them but remake and reformulate political messages and try to come to grips with new situations based on their own experiences and knowledge.[8] This might prove to be the most important reason the revolution has lasted as long as it has.

As we have seen, personal experiences contribute significantly to political ideology. Whether a person had a hard life before the revolution and participated in building the new society is important to that person's view of Cuban society today. These experiences have given many people a deep feeling for the revolution and their society, and they feel that the revolution is worth struggling for. Many Palmerans said in the summer of 1993 that they would not give up. What they meant was that they had invested so much time, effort, and ideals in the revolution that giving up would mean throwing everything away. In other words, in many ways they have internalized everything the revolution stands for.

Those who have been negative toward the revolution also trust their own experiences, which have been confirmed by the deterioration in their standards of living. Their views of Cuban society have become more extreme, their ranks are more numerous, and their opinions are expressed more harshly. Teresa has never been a loyal revolutionary, but she has usually acknowledged the benefits of the system. In the summer of 1993 when we were watching a TV program in which a historical account was given of the victories of the rebel army and the feats of the revolution, Teresa spat out her bitter comment: "They talk about the revolution, what it has given us. I want to puke. Look at me, I have no clothes, I'm always hungry, and I live in a pig sty. What has the revolution given

[8]This resembles what Ulf Hannerz (1992) calls the creolization of transcultural phenomena. He argues that people do not just accept cultural messages from large cultural centers but reformulate them by incorporating aspects of their own culture.

me?" She was not interested in analyzing the situation or in understanding it; she had once again gotten proof for her opinion that the revolution *no sirve* (was no good). The explanations Palmerans usually give for why Cuba is in the midst of a special period are quite uniform and consist of references to the U.S. embargo and the disintegration of the Soviet Union and the socialist states in Eastern Europe. Not everyone has been able to accept the difficult economic situation, and a handful of people have left Palmera to go to Canada, Jamaica, or the United States. "Se fue" is the grim expression, often said with sorrow and grief, that family members who have stayed use.[9]

As mentioned earlier, the discrepancies between the rhetoric and the reality have long been part of the criticism Cubans level at their leaders. Nowadays when leaders maintain that Cuba is still "the best" in most respects, most people think it sounds false. When Cuba's standard of living was fairly high, it could always be said that even if people lacked freedom or alternatives, no one went hungry or sick for lack of money. One no longer hears this argument. It seems, however, that the leaders are also changing their rhetoric to fit the current situation. In the closing speech of the 1995 world meeting of Solidarity with Cuba for example, instead of talking about acts, Fidel Castro talked about principles: "For us principles are worth more than our own life." He went on to say that "we have to save the conquests of socialism, because we cannot say in these moments that we are building socialism" (*Liberación*, 17 Feb. 1995). This is quite different from what Fidel and other leaders said during the time of my fieldwork, when the catch words were "act," "struggle,"

[9]During the special period there has been growing polarization in Cuban society. More people are critical of and discontent with the political system, although there are still people who are loyal to and defend the socialist system. In the 1980s, there were those who were loyal to the Party and the revolution, those who accepted the situation but were quite indifferent to the politics, and those who were against the political system (see IRELA 1994; Baloyra 1993: chap. 3). During my fieldwork in Palmera, the middle group seemed to be the biggest, the first group was rather big, and the third group was small. In the country as a whole, I would guess that the first and the third groups were about equally big and that the middle group also was the biggest. Today the opinions of Palmerans probably more closely resemble national opinions.

and "build." To ask people to sacrifice more would be an insult, since all Cubans today are sacrificing more than ever just by going about their daily lives.

The idea that the Cuban revolution is perpetual has been pushed to the background. On the whole, there seems to be less talk about the revolution. Today the discourse of both the leaders and the people is more pragmatic. Necessities govern. More than ever, what is most important is to survive and to find solutions to daily problems. People must take initiatives and are encouraged by their leaders to do so. Some people are trying to profit from whatever they can, while many do not like the new way of life but are adapting and making the best of it. The folk versions of socialist ideology have taken on greater meaning. The finer points of Marxism-Leninism have never been of great interest to ordinary people. Today the leaders also play down these points and highlight the ideas promoted by José Martí—the importance of independence, dignity, humanity, and social justice.[10]

That patriotic feelings still are strong could be seen in the spring of 1995, when the Helms-Burton law was proposed in the United States. It suggested that Cubans who left their country after 1959 should be able to claim their property when they return to Cuba. This made most Cubans furious and worried. Meetings were shown on television in which people angrily shouted that if anyone believed that they could come and take "my house," "my hospital," or "my day care center" away, they were sadly mistaken. And the anger and worry were expressed not just in organized meetings. People often mentioned in casual conversations that they felt that the law was an

[10]On 19 May 1995, a ceremony commemorating the centenary of José Martí's death in battle was held at Dos Ríos, in the province of Granma. The celebrations seemed symbolically to suggest political modifications. Carlos Lage, the young and popular vice president, gave the main speech while Fidel sat behind him on the podium. Lage, who is one of the important new politicians, started his speech by addressing the comandante as "Querido Fidel," an unusual intimacy in a formal situation. He spoke about the value of the ideas of Martí in furthering the revolution and about the difficult economic times, which had required changes but which would not lead to capitalism. He also extended a hand to more liberal Cuban-Americans while firmly criticizing Jorge Mas Canosa and his group, as well as the proposed Helms-Burton law (*Granma*, 20 May 1995).

impertinence and a crime that they would never allow to materialize. What most leaders and other people seem to agree on is that it is important to safeguard the social benefits of the last thirty-five years—the social justice, free medical care, access to schooling, and jobs for everyone. Some of these benefits, which many Cubans have taken for granted, such as jobs and free or inexpensive medicine for everyone, have already been lost and others are at risk. The events of the last several years have shown people that the benefits are vulnerable and it is vital to protect them.

References

Agar, Michael. 1980. *The Professional Stranger: An Informal Introduction to Ethnography*. San Diego: Academic Press.

Almeida Bosque, Juan. 1989. *La Sierra*. Havana: Editora Politica.

Althusser, Louis. 1971. Ideology and Ideological State Apparatuses (Notes towards an Investigation). In Louis Althusser, *Lenin and Philosophy and Other Essays*, 127–86. New York: Monthly Review Press.

Arguelles, Lourdes, and Ruby B. Rich. 1984. Homosexuality, Homophobia, and Revolution: Notes toward an Understanding of the Cuban Lesbian and Gay Male Experience, Part I. *Signs* 9:683–99.

Baloyra, Enrique A. 1993. Socialist Transitions and Prospects for Change in Cuba. In Enrique A. Baloyra and James A. Morris, eds., *Conflict and Change in Cuba*, 38–63. Albuquerque: University of New Mexico Press.

Bengelsdorf, Carollee. 1988. On the Problem of Studying Women in Cuba. In Andrew Zimbalist ed., *Cuban Political Economy: Controversies in Cubanology*, 119–36. Boulder, Colo.: Westview Press.

——. 1994. *The Problem of Democracy in Cuba: Between Vision and Reality*. New York: Oxford University Press.

Bohman, Kristina. 1984. *Women in the Barrio: Class and Gender in a Colombian City*. Stockholm: Stockholm Studies in Social Anthropology.

Bourdieu, Pierre. 1977. *Outline of a Theory of Practice*. Cambridge: Cambridge University Press.

Brenner, Philip, et al., eds. 1989. *The Cuba Reader: The Making of a Revolutionary Society*. New York: Grove Press.

Brundenius, Claes. 1984. *Revolutionary Cuba: The Challenge of Economic Growth with Equity*. London: Heinemann.

Butterworth, Douglas. 1974. Grass-Roots Political Organization in Cuba: A Case of the Committees for the Defense of the Revolution. In Wayne A. Cornelius and Felicity M. Trueblood, eds., *Latin American Urban Research.* Anthropological Perspectives on Latin American Urbanization, 4:183–203. Beverly Hills: Sage.

——. 1980. *People of Buena Ventura: Relocation of Slum Dwellers in Postrevolutionary Cuba.* Urbana: University of Illinois Press.

Caplan, Pat. 1993. Socialism from above in Tanzania: The View from Below. In Chris M. Hann, ed., *Socialism. Ideals, Ideologies, and Local Practice,* 77–91. London: Routledge.

Cardoso, Eliana, and Ann Helwege. 1992. *Cuba after Communism.* Cambridge: MIT Press.

Casal, Lourdes. 1980. Revolution and Conciencia: Women in Cuba. In Carol R. Berkin and Clara M. Lovett, eds., *Women, War and Revolution,* 183–206. New York: Holmes & Meier.

Castro, Fidel. 1983. *La Historia me Absolverá.* Havana: Editorial de Ciencias Sociales.

——. 1988. *La Revolución Cubana: Una Proeza Extraordinaria.* Havana: Editoria Politica.

Cohen, Abner. 1979. Political Symbolism. *Annual Review of Anthropology* 8:87–113.

Collins Spanish Concise Dictionary. 1990. London: Collins.

Connerton, Paul. 1989. *How Societies Remember.* Cambridge: Cambridge University Press.

Cuba, Territorio Libre de Analfabetismo. 1981. Havana: Editorial de Ciencias Sociales.

Daniel, Yvonne. 1995. *Rumba Dance and Social Change in Contemporary Cuba.* Bloomington: Indiana University Press.

Deutschmann, David, ed. 1987. *Che Guevara and the Cuban Revolution: Writings and Speeches of Ernesto Che Guevara.* Sydney: Pathfinder/Pacific and Asia.

di Leonardo, Micaela, ed. 1991. *Gender at the Crossroads of Knowledge: Feminist Anthropology in the Postmodern Era.* Berkeley: University of California Press.

Domínguez, Jorge. 1978. *Cuba: Order and Revolution.* Cambridge: Harvard University Press.

Eckstein, Susan Eva. 1994. *Back from the Future: Cuba under Castro.* Princeton: Princeton University Press.

Ekman, Ann-Kristin. 1991. *Community, Carnival and Campaign: Expressions of Belonging in a Swedish Region.* Stockholm: Stockholm Studies in Social Anthropology.

Estatutos del Partido Comunista de Cuba. 1986. Havana: Editora Politica.

Evans, Grant. 1993. Buddhism and Economic Action in Socialist Laos. In Chris

M. Hann, ed., *Socialism. Ideals, Ideologies, and Local Practice*, 132–47. London: Routledge.

Feinsilver, Julie. 1989. Cuba as a "World Medical Power": The Politics of Symbolism. *Latin American Research Review* 24:1–34.

Fernandez, Enrique. 1991. Fidel's Limbo. *Condé Nast Traveler*, July, 72–126.

Fonseca, Claudia. 1991. Spouses, Siblings and Sex-Linked Bonding: A Look at Kinship Organization in a Brazilian Slum. In Elizabeth Jelin, ed., *Family, Household and Gender Relations in Latin America*, 133–60. London: Kegan Paul International.

Geertz, Clifford. 1973. *The Interpretation of Cultures*. New York: Basic Books.

Gilmore, David. 1980. *The People of the Plain*. New York: Columbia University Press.

——. 1990. *Manhood in the Making: Cultural Concepts of Masculinity*. New Haven: Yale University Press.

Gilmore, Margaret, and David Gilmore. 1979. "Machismo": A Psychodynamic Approach (Spain). *Journal of Psychological Anthropology* 2:281–99.

Gissi Bustos, Jorge. 1976. Mythology about Women, with Special Reference to Chile. In June Nash and Helen Safa, eds., *Sex and Class in Latin America*, 30–45. New York: Praeger.

Goñi, José, ed. 1987. *Olof Palme. Suecia y América Latina. Antología de Documentos Políticos*. Buenos Aires: Puntosur editores y Stockholm: LAIS.

Gramsci, Antonio. 1971. *Selections from the Prison Notebooks*. London: Lawrence and Wishart.

Gudeman, Stephen, and Alberto Rivera. 1990. *Conversations in Colombia: The Domestic Economy in Life and Text*. Cambridge: Cambridge University Press.

Guevara, Ernesto "Che." 1971. *Reminiscenses of the Cuban Revolutionary War*. New York: Monthly Review Press.

Hann, Chris M., ed. 1993. *Socialism. Ideals, Ideologies, and Local Practice*. London: Routledge.

Hannerz, Ulf. 1992. *Cultural Complexity: Studies in the Social Organization of Meaning*. New York: Columbia University Press.

Hannerz, Ulf, Rita Liljeström, and Orvar Löfgren, eds. 1982. *Culture and Consciousness: An Interdisciplinary Analysis* (in Swedish). Stockholm: Akademilitteratur.

Hart, Keith. 1973. Informal Income Opportunities and Urban Employment in Ghana. *Journal of Modern African Studies* 11:61–89.

Herzfeld, Michael. 1987. "As in Your Own House": Hospitality, Ethnography, and the Stereotype of Mediterranean Society. In David Gilmore, ed., *Honor and Shame and the Unity of the Mediterranean*, 75–89. Washington D.C.: American Anthropological Association.

Hijuelos, Oscar. 1989. *The Mambo Kings Play Songs of Love*. London: Penguin Books.

Hugh-Jones, Stephen. 1992. Yesterday's Luxuries, Tomorrow's Necessities: Business and Barter in Northwest Amazonia. In Caroline Humphrey and Stephen Hugh-Jones, eds., *Barter, Exchange and Value: An Anthropological Approach*, 42–74. Cambridge: Cambridge University Press.

Humphrey, Caroline, and Stephen Hugh-Jones. 1992. Introduction: Barter, Exchange and Value. In Caroline Humphrey and Stephen Hugh-Jones, eds., *Barter, Exchange and Value: An Anthropological Approach*, 1–20. Cambridge: Cambridge University Press.

IRELA. 1994. Cuba in Crisis: Processes and Prospects. Dossier no. 50. Madrid. September. Typescript.

Isbell, Billie Jean. 1978. *To Defend Ourselves: Ecology and Ritual in an Andean Village*. Austin: University of Texas Press.

Jelin, Elizabeth. 1991a. Family and Household: Outside World and Private Life. In Elizabeth Jelin, ed., *Family, Household and Gender Relations in Latin America,* 165–96. London: Kegan Paul International.

——.1991b. Social Relations of Consumption: The Urban Popular Household. In Elizabeth Jelin, ed., *Family, Household and Gender Relations in Latin America,* 12–39. London: Kegan Paul International.

Jørgensen, Bård. 1980. "Political Participation in the Socialist Transformation of Cuba: The Role of the Organs of People's Power" (in Norwegian). Thesis in Human Geography. Bergen: Geografisk Institutt, University of Bergen. Typescript.

——. 1983. The Interrelationship between Base and Superstructure in Cuba. *Ibero Americana: Nordic Journal of Latin American Studies* 13:27–42.

Kapcia, Antoni. 1992. *The Cuban Revolution in Crisis*. London: Research Institute for the Study of Conflict and Terrorism.

Kapferer, Bruce. 1988. *Legends of People: Myths of State*. Washington, D.C.: Smithsonian Institution Press.

Keesing, Roger M. 1987. Models, "Folk" and "Cultural": Paradigms Regained? In Dorothy Holland and Naomi Quinn, eds., *Cultural Models in Language and Thought*, 369–93. New York: Cambridge University Press.

Kideckel, David. 1983. Secular Ritual and Social Change: A Romanian Case. *Anthropological Quarterly* 56:52–75.

Lancaster, Roger. 1988. *Thanks to God and the Revolution: Popular Religion and Class Consciousness in the New Nicaragua*. New York: Columbia University Press.

——. 1992. *Life Is Hard: Machismo, Danger, and the Intimacy of Power in Nicaragua*. Berkeley: University of California Press.

Lane, Christel. 1981. *The Rites of Rulers: Rituals in Industrial Society: The Soviet Case*. Cambridge: Cambridge University Press.

Larguia, Isabel, and John Dumoulin. 1985. Women's Equality and the Cuban Revolution. In June Nash and Helen Safa, eds., *Women and Change in Latin America*, 344–68. South Hadley, Massachusetts: Bergin and Garvey.

Latin American and Caribbean Women's Collective. 1977. *Slaves of Slaves: The Challenge of Latin American Women*. London: Zed Press.

Leach, Edmund. 1976. *Culture and Communication*. Cambridge: Cambridge University Press.

Leahy, Margaret. 1986. *Development Strategies and the Status of Women: A Comparative Study of the United States, Mexico, the Soviet Union and Cuba*. Boulder, Colo.: Lynne Rienner.

Leiner, Marvin. 1994. *Sexual Politics in Cuba: Machismo, Homosexuality, and AIDS*. Boulder, Colo.: Westview Press.

Lenin, Vladimir. 1964. *The State and the Revolution* (in Swedish). Stockholm: Rabén och Sjögren.

——. 1974. *What Is To Be Done?* (in Swedish). In Selected Works in Three Volumes: Part I. Stockholm: Arbetarkultur.

Lewis, Oscar, Ruth Lewis, and Susan Rigdon. 1977a. *Four Men: Living the Revolution. An Oral History of Contemporary Cuba*. Urbana: University of Illinois Press.

——. 1977b. *Four Women: Living the Revolution. An Oral History of Contemporary Cuba*. Urbana: University of Illinois Press.

——. 1978. *Neighbors: Living the Revolution. An Oral History of Contemporary Cuba*. Urbana: University of Illinois Press.

Lockwood, Lee. 1990. *Castro's Cuba, Cuba's Fidel*. Boulder, Colo.: Westview Press.

Martínez Alier, Verena. 1972. Elopement and Seduction in Nineteenth-Century Cuba. *Past and Present* 55:91–129.

Mauss, Marcel. 1969. *The Gift. Forms and Functions of Exchange in Archaic Societies*. London: Routledge.

Miller, Tom. 1992. *Trading with the Enemy: A Yankee Travels through Castro's Cuba*. New York: Atheneum.

Molyneux, Maxine. 1981. Socialist Societies Old and New: Progress Towards Women's Emancipation? *Feminist Review* 8:1–34.

Moore, Henrietta. 1988. *Feminism and Anthropology*. Oxford: Polity Press.

Moore, Sally Falk. 1977. Political Meetings and the Simulation of Unanimity: Kilimanjaro 1973. In Sally Falk Moore and Barbara Myerhoff, eds., *Secular Ritual*, 151–72. Assen: Van Gorcum.

Murray, Nicola. 1979. Socialism and Feminism: Women and the Cuban Revolution, Part I. *Feminist Review* 2:57–73.

Nelson, Lowry. 1950. *Rural Cuba*. Minneapolis: University of Minnesota Press.

Oppenheimer, Andres. 1992. *Castro's Final Hour. The Secret Story behind the Coming Downfall of Communist Cuba*. New York: Simon and Schuster.

Paine, Robert, ed. 1981. *Politically Speaking: Cross-Cultural Studies of Rhetoric*. St. Johns, Newfoundland: Institute of Social and Economic Research, Memorial University.

Páz, Senel. 1994. *El Lobo, el Bosque y el Hombre Nuevo*. Sancti Spíritus, Cuba: Ediciones Luminaria.

Pérez, Louis A., Jr. 1988. *Cuba: Between Reform and Revolution*. Oxford: Oxford University Press.

Pérez-López, Jorge F. 1989. Wages, Earnings, Hours of Work, and Retail Prices in Cuba. *Cuban Studies* 19: 199–224.

Pérez-Stable, Marifeli. 1993. *The Cuban Revolution: Origins, Course and Legacy*. Oxford: Oxford University Press.

Potter, Jack M., and Sulamith Heins Potter. 1990. *China's Peasants: The Anthropology of a Revolution*. New York: Cambridge University Press.

Powdermaker, Hortense. 1966. *Stranger and Friend: The Way of an Anthropologist*. New York: Norton.

Programa del Partido Comunista de Cuba. 1987. Havana: Editora Politica.

Randall, Margaret. 1981. *Women in Cuba: Twenty Years Later*. New York: Smyrna Press.

Rassi, Reynold. 1981. *Cuba: Nueva División Político-Administrativa*. Havana: Editorial Orbe.

Ravenet Ramirez, Mariana, Niurka Pérez Rojas, and Marta Toledo Fraga. 1989. *La Mujer Rural y Urbana: Estudios de Casos*. Havana: Editorial de Ciencias Sociales.

Reed, Gail. 1992. *Island in the Storm: The Cuban Communist Party's Fourth Congress*. Melbourne: Ocean Press.

Rosaldo, Michelle, and Louise Lamphere, eds. 1974. *Women, Culture and Society*. Stanford: Stanford University Press.

Rosendahl, Mona. 1985. *Conflict and Compliance: Class Consciousness among Swedish Workers*. Stockholm: Stockholm Studies in Social Anthropology 14.

——. 1992a. The March of History: Revolution as Development in Cuba. In Gudrun Dahl and Annika Rabo, eds., *Kam-ap or Take-off: Local Notions of Development*, 69–97. Stockholm: Stockholm Studies in Social Anthropology.

——. 1992b. Historia e Identidad Revolucionaria en Cuba. In America Latina Local y Regional. *Estudios y Memorias* 6:33–42. Volume 3, CESLA, University of Warsaw.

——. 1997. The Ever-Changing Revolution. In Mona Rosendahl, ed., *The Current Situation in Cuba: Challenges and Alternatives*. Stockholm: Institute of Latin American Studies.

Rosenthal, Marguerite. 1992. The Problem of Single Motherhood in Cuba. In Sandor Halebsky and John M. Kirk, eds., *Cuba in Transition: Crisis and Transformation*, 161–75. Boulder, Colo.: Westview Press.

Rosling, Hans. 1994. Unbalanced Diet behind Epidemic in Cuba: Smoking Risk Factor for Optical Neuropathy (in Swedish). *Läkartidningen* 44:4018–19.

Sahlins, Marshall. 1972. *Stone Age Economics*. London: Tavistock.

Saltzman Chafetz, Janet. 1991. The Gender Division of Labor and the Reproduction of Female Disadvantage: Toward an Integrated Theory. In Rae Lesser Blumberg, ed., *Gender, Family, and Economy: The Triple Overlap*, 74–94. Newbury Park, Calif.: Sage.

Scheper-Hughes, Nancy. 1992. *Death without Weeping: The Violence of Everyday Life in Brazil.* Berkeley: University of California Press.

Scott, James C. 1985. *Weapons of the Weak: Everyday Forms of Peasant Resistance*. New Haven: Yale University Press.

Shostak, Marjorie. 1990. *Nisa: The Life and Words of a !Kung Woman*. London: Earthscan Publications.

Smith, M. Estellie. 1989. The Informal Economy. In Stuart Plattner, ed., *Economic Anthropology*, 292–463. Stanford: Stanford University Press.

Smith, Lois M. 1992. Sexuality and Socialism in Cuba. In Sandor Halebsky and John M. Kirk, eds., *Cuba in Transition: Crisis and Transformation*, 177–91. Boulder, Colo.: Westview Press.

Smith, Lois M., and Alfred Padula. 1988. Women Workers in Socialist Cuba, 1959–1988: Progress and Problems. *Ibero-Americana: Nordic Journal of Latin American Studies* 18:33–55.

Smith, Raymond. 1988. *Kinship and Class in the West Indies: A Genealogical Study of Jamaica and Guyana*. Cambridge: Cambridge University Press.

Stack, Carol. 1974. *All Our Kin: Stategies for Survival in a Black Community*. New York: Harper.

Stone, Elizabeth, ed. 1981. *Women and the Cuban Revolution*. New York: Pathfinder Press.

Stoner, Lynn K. 1991. *From the House to the Streets: The Cuban Woman's Movement for Legal Reform, 1898–1940*. Durham: Duke University Press.

Sutherland, Elisabeth. 1969. *The Youngest Revolution*. New York: Dial Press.

Therborn, Göran. 1981. *The Ideology of Power and the Power of Ideology* (in Swedish). Stockholm: Zenit Förlag.

Thompson, John B. 1990. *Ideology and Modern Culture: Critical Social Theory in the Era of Mass Communication*. Oxford: Polity Press.

Thompson, Kenneth. 1986. *Beliefs and Ideology*. London: Tavistock.

Valdés, Nelson P. 1992. Cuban Political Culture: Between Betrayal and Death. In Sandor Halebsky and John M. Kirk, eds., *Cuba in Transition: Crisis and Transformation*, 207–28. Boulder, Colo.: Westview Press.

Vindicación de Cuba. 1989. Havana: Editora Politica.

Waller, Michael. 1981. *Democratic Socialism: An Historical Commentary*. Manchester: Manchester University Press.

Whitehead, Tony Larry. 1986. Breakdown, Resolution, and Coherence: The Fieldwork of a Big, Brown, Pretty-Talking Man in a West Indian Community. In Tony Larry Whitehead and Mary Ellen Conaway, eds., *Self, Sex and Gender in Cross-Cultural Fieldwork*, 213–39. Urbana: University of Illinois Press.

Williams, Raymond. 1977. *Marxism and Literature*. Oxford: Oxford University Press.

Wilson, Peter J. 1973. *Crab Antics: The Social Anthropology of English-Speaking Negro Societies of the Caribbean*. New Haven: Yale University Press.

Yang Mei-hui, Mayfair. 1988. The Modernity of Power in the Chinese Socialist Order. *Cultural Anthropology* 3:408–29.

Yglesias, José. 1968. *In the Fist of the Revolution: Life in a Cuban Country Town*. New York: Random House.

Zimbalist, Andrew. 1989. Incentives and Planning in Cuba. *Latin American Research Review* 24:65–93.

Index

Anthropology of Contemporary Issues

A SERIES EDITED BY

ROGER SANJEK

Chinatown No More: Taiwan Immigrants in Contemporary New York
BY HSIANG-SHUI CHEN

Farm Work and Fieldwork: American Agriculture in Anthropological Perspective
EDITED BY MICHAEL CHIBNIK

The Varieties of Ethnic Experience: Kinship, Class, and Gender among California Italian-Americans
BY MICAELA DI LEONARDO

Lord, I'm Coming Home: Everyday Aesthetics in Tidewater North Carolina
BY JOHN FORREST

Chinese Working-Class Lives: Getting By in Taiwan
BY HILL GATES

Accommodation without Assimilation: Sikh Immigrants in an American High School
BY MARGARET A. GIBSON

Praying for Justice: Faith, Order, and Community in an American Town
BY CAROL J. GREENHOUSE

Distant Companions: Servants and Employers in Zambia, 1900–1985
BY KAREN TRANBERG HANSEN

Rx: Spiritist as Needed: A study of a Puerto Rican Community Mental Health Resource
BY ALAN HARWOOD

Dismantling Apartheid: A South African Town in Transition
BY WALTON R. JOHNSON

Caribbean New York: Black Immigrants and the Politics of Race
BY PHILIP KASINITZ

The Solitude of Collectivism: Romanian Villagers to the Revolution and Beyond
BY DAVID A. KIDECKEL

Nuclear Summer: The Clash of Communities at the Seneca Women's Peace Encampment
BY LOUISE KRASNIEWICZ

Between Two Worlds: Ethnographic Essays on American Jewry
EDITED BY JACK KUGELMASS

American Odyssey: Haitians in New York City
by Michel S. Laguerre
Sunbelt Working Mothers: Reconciling Family and Factory
by Louise Lamphere, Patricia Zavella, Felipe Gonzales and Peter B. Evans
Creativity/Anthropology
editied by Smadar Lavie, Kirin Narayan and Renato Rosaldo
Cities, Classes, and the Social Order
by Anthony Leeds, edited by Roger Sanjek
Lesbian Mothers: Accounts of Gender in American Culture
by Ellen Lewin
Civilized Women: Gender and Prestige in Southeastern Liberia
by Mary H. Moran
Blood, Sweat, and Mahjong: Family and Enterprise in an Overseas Chinese Community
by Ellen Oxfeld
The Magic City: Unemployment in a Working-Class Community
by Gregory Pappas
The Korean American Dream: Immigrants and Small Business in New York City
by Kyeyoung Park
Inside the Revolution: Everyday Life in Socialist Cuba
by Mona Rosendahl
State and Family in Singapore: Restructuring an Industrial Society
by Janet W. Salaff
Uneasy Endings: Daily Life in an American Nursing Home
by Renée Rose Shield
Children of Circumstances: Israeli Emigrants in New York
by Moshe Shokeid
History and Power in the Study of Law: New Directions in Legal Anthropology
editied by June Starr and Jane F. Collier
"Getting Paid": Youth Crime and Work in the Inner City
by Mercer L. Sullivan
Breaking the Silence: Redress and Japanese American Ethnicity
by Yasuko I. Takezawa
Underground Harmonies: Music and Politics in the Subways of New York
by Susie J. Tanenbaum
City of Green Benches: Growing Old in a New Downtown
by Maria D. Vesperi

Strawberry Fields: Politics, Class, and Work in California Agriculture
BY MIRIAM J. WELLS
Renunciation and Reformulation: A study of Conversion in an American Sect
BY HARRIET WHITEHEAD
Upscaling Downtown: Stalled Gentrification in Washington, D.C.
BY BRETT WILLIAMS
Women's Work and Chicano Families: Cannery Workers of the Santa Clara Valley
BY PATRICIA ZAVELLA